GREAT RIVER LEGS

LAURA MADELINE WISEMAN

Zea Books, Lincoln, Nebraska

Great River Legs

ISBN 978-1-60962-203-9

Zea Books are published by the University of Nebraska-Lincoln Libraries

Electronic (pdf) editions available online at http://digitalcommons.unl.edu/zeabooks/
Print edition available from http://www.lulu.com/spotlight/unlib

UNL does not discriminate based upon any protected status.
Please go to http://www.unl.edu/equity/notice-nondiscrimination

for Adam

*It's as though we've spent our lives on a bicycle, pedaling
hard to get away from the present moment. We pedal
to resist what is happening, we pedal
to try to make something happen, we pedal
to get somewhere else. The more we feel like something
is missing or something is WRONG, the faster we pedal.
Even in the midst of a meditation we might realize we are pedaling
—striving to be with the breath, chasing after a fantasy.*

—Tara Brach

TABLE OF CONTENTS

3

INTRODUCTION

Great River Legs is a lyric collection of prose poetry, creative nonfiction, and found poetry. This creative response documents my 1,398 mile, 25-day bicycle ride from Muscatine, Iowa, to Baton Rouge, Louisiana, between October 2017 – March 2018. The journey took place in legs over breaks during the school year, with two additional back-to-back weekend rides that started the adventure.

Born and raised in Iowa, I rode with my friends, siblings, and cousins—big wheels, tricycles, bicycles with training wheels, and hand-me-down ten-speeds. When I got my first part-time job washing dishes in a nursing home, my dad gave me his sister's old Olympia Huffy as a commuter. In graduate school, I upgraded to a hybrid. After earning a Ph.D. in English and riding a hybrid during my first year on RAGBRAI, I bought my first entry-level road bike, a Trek Lexa. In 2017, I completed my first cross-country bicycle journey, from Astoria, Oregon, to Yorktown, Virginia, in 60 days, pedaling 4,200 miles with a support driver, my husband. After we returned, I wanted to find ways to cycle during the school year beyond commuting. Would it be possible to complete a long-distance journey in legs through the colder months of autumn, winter, and spring? I started planning a bike trip along the great rivers that hugged the state of Iowa and beyond.

Two back-to-back weekend bike trips in October served as testers. Tests passed, I decided to try the whole route. In October and on Thanksgiving break, I pedaled Muscatine, Iowa, to Cape Girardeau, Missouri. A few brisk morning rides required strategic layers while offering the golden wonder of the Midwest, post-harvest. Shortened days and work calls made for low mileage while listening to audiobooks added a literary, journalistic, and meditative hue of context and place. During winter break, I biked Baton Rouge, Louisiana, to Bucksnort, Tennessee. The southern states welcomed, balmy, lush, and percussive with thunderstorms. The Natchez Trace Parkway greeted with historical markers, kind stewards, and a century. Spring Break's miles meant linking the two routes, with a few bonus trips between. On one bonus leg, I attempted my first solo self-supported ride on another section of the Natchez, a ride I later wrote about in my book *Safety Measures*.

Throughout the ride, I had support. My husband drove, arranged accommodations, and found attractions—Jesse James Cave, breweries, Louisiana State Capitol, local eateries. Together we took a self-guided tour of Mark Twain's hometown, chatted with greeters on the Trace, and cruised the Land Between the Lakes.

Throughout, the job dominated. The short days meant I worked several hours pre-dawn. I worked after the ride. I worked when it wasn't my turn to drive. When I pedaled, the audiobooks too focused on work, whatever the genre, and became a moving meditation on riverfront economics, local industry, community, and place. Having grown up in Des Moines where two rivers crossed, it added context to the rivers of my childhood.

I collected data with a smartwatch and cyclometer and logged the data points in a spreadsheet and online. Research during and after the ride added to the record keeping. I kept a journal upon which this book is based. To make a book means making a story, structure, and order of experience. This book is creative – prose poetry, creative nonfiction, found poetry, a story. It is from my memories, and if I misinterpreted an intention or a situation, I am sorry. My intent was human, kind, and compassionate storytelling. The book's structure follows the legs of the journey. Each leg and day include a data chart. The appendices include summation data charts on land, mileage, and waterways. The legs open with a found poem in the form of adversaria, highlighting phrases and words on mindfulness and meditation.

Biking the great river in legs during one school year treated me to a long-distance education. Over the following summer, I linked by bicycle Muscatine, Iowa, to the Mississippi headwaters at Itasca State Park in Minnesota. Looking at a map of such rivers humbles me—their size, scope, reach. Following them through the places that thrive along their shores in the mindful movement of cycling is the journey that inspires the next. I'm grateful.

Laura Madeline Wiseman, Ph.D.
Lincoln, Nebraska
October 2021

A PATH

But without a doubt, **our simple** breathing meditation contains the seed of enlightenment. The emphasis is on mindfulness and awareness of breathing, the **path** to tranquility and insight. No details, **no map**, no companions, **no guide, just** a direction and **a desire** in response **to** an overriding imperative from within: **go home**. It is very much like that on the journey to meditation too. No matter how many mystics **we read**, we cannot **move forward on** the spiritual **path** without practic**in**g their **teaching** in daily life. Remember that in letting go of distraction, the important word is gentle. We can gently let go. We can forgive ourselves for **having wandered**, and with great kindness to ourselves, **we** can **begin again**. Self-knowledge is acquired through an altogether different way of knowing, one in which the mind is engaged in being. This is meditation—the **path** we are about to explore. There are many **paths** that lead towards enlightenment. Some of these **paths** lead all the way, while others take a pilgrim only a little way. **Some paths are** steep and **dangerous**; others slow and gentle. This is a **difficult** path, calling for tremendous powers of will and clarity of mind. **To stay with that** shakiness—to stay with a **broken** heart, with a **rumbling** stomach, with the feeling of hopelessness and **wanting** to get revenge—that is the **path** of true awakening. Yoga **asks us to look** at the unfolding complexities of consciousness on the evolutionary **path** that are even more subtle—such as mind, "I-shape," and intelligence—**and to question** what they are and how **they work**. Your blossoming will need to be **unlike anyone else's**; just as every double helix of DNA is unique, so is every person's **path**.

FALL LEGS

Muscatine, IA to Cape Girardeau, MO

Fall

Highest/Lowest Temperature (°F)	78/24
Most Precipitation (inches)	0
Highest/Lowest Max Wind (MPH)	26/0
Longest/Shortest Day Length	10h 40m/9h 40m
Earliest/Latest Sunrise	6:37/7:34
Earliest/Latest Sunset	4:43/6:09

States: Iowa, Missouri, & Illinois

Rivers: Iowa, Mississippi, Cuivre, Salt, Des Moines, Meramec, Big, Flat, St. Francis, Little St. Francis, Castor, & White Water

FIRST, THE IOWA TO TEST OUR LEGS

"I'll drive the first leg," you say, to get me going on this river route and find tonight's camp.

"Sunset is 6:04 here," I say. How did I convince you to sneak off in October? Do I really get three hours until dark? I want to ride, and you, to find the beer.

We find Burlington, then Bluff Road. Industry roads converge at the riverfront. "Are we allowed to park here?" I ask.

You cut the engine. A worker inside a truck lifts his gaze towards our getaway car. I duck into the backseat, swapping work clothes for cycling ones. You ready my bicycle, Ganga.

"Bye." I shake your hand.

"Bye." You give mine a squeeze, holding on. You never want to go. I always want to. Why are we so weird?

Burlington, IA to Port Louisa, IA

October 16

Temperature (°F)	74/41
Precipitation (inches)	0
Max Wind (MPH)	24
Day Length	10h 40m
Sunrise/Sunset	7:29/6:09

Iowa River, Mississippi River, & Yellow Spring Creek

You drive along the Mississippi bends with our camping gear, a copy of the map, and a hankering for uncommon stouts. When you find a local pub with a ghost walk, patrons loiter with laughter, tipping beers named *Undercurrent*, *Paddle Wheel*, and *Mississippi*. You follow them through the darkness, then search for me somewhere ahead.

Meanwhile, I ride my bicycle towards Muscatine and its dogs. The miles keep coming, and I get them all—Burlington, Kingston, Oakville, Toolesboro. Some cornfields stand shorn, their rows trimmed to stalks pegging the soil like monks. Others clack leaves, raspy dimness through which to step. The brisk wind shifts the hills with ochre. The light fades as the miles accrue. In the shush, the audiobook plays.

When we meet at home after a commute, I often ask, "What are you reading?"

Earbuds bounce like pearls at your throat. You tuck them into your jacket and say, "NPR, a podcast," or last summer's book on job loss to automation, *"Rise of the Robots."*

If you would've asked, I would've said, *A memoir on yoga in Fairfield, Iowa.* Instead, I practice my response, just in case. We both grew up in Iowa. If the author hails from another town, the landscape remains the same. She grew up with Ayurveda, mantras, and Vedic science, her dad a poet, her mom a meditator. If the townies sneered, *Flyers,* her mom worked every kind of job. Money worries and Iowa's winter slid through the windows, and her first mantra drummed.

When you find me, I say, "I want to meditate."

A CHERRY TO CUIVRE

We teach our classes. Last weekend we attended a conference, and this weekend, we will attend another. When I asked you if we could slip a bike ride between then, you said, "Okay." If tailed, what information would someone gather about us? We work and read. I ride my bike. You drink local beer.

"Make sure no one looks." I angle the rearview mirror at the road to catch invaders, then switch car clothes for bicycle ones. Jersey on, I ask, "Meet you in Troy?"

You drive ahead to find tonight's camp, and I ride twelve miles towards epic poetry and myth. My audiobook says Iowa, meditation, and calm. The map directs, *Continue straight.* This Day 2 tests another leg of biking the great rivers that head south. When I asked you if we might, you said, "We always tire dip the Missouri and Mississippi on RAGBRAI." Could we follow the Mississippi from Muscatine, Iowa, to Cape Girardeau, Missouri, by bicycle? And if so, what assumptions about our waterways would this disabuse?

In Troy, the line of storm grates along the cemetery answers with nothing, mute with a hunger for bicycle tires. Do the buried hunger for a bicycle? The full moon answers, *Nowhere here,* and I get it—quiet mind, cessation of thought, breath. I ready to be river dipped, chase apples for love, and portend which lands will fall or rise.

We rendezvous with a kiss, then drive to camp. I do moon salutes, then bring you a beer from the cooler. "Bottle opener?" I ask.

Wright City, MO to Troy, MO	
All Soul's Day	
Temperature (°F)	78/53
Precipitation (inches)	0
Max Wind (MPH)	16
Day Length	10h 31m
Sunrise/Sunset	7:33/6:04
Cuivre River & Big Creek	

"No, but there's a way."

THE MISSISSIPPI OR THE MISSOURI

Cuivre River State Park is ours. Outdoors, you roll around all night. Outdoors, I sleep like a little girl. Why are we so weird?

I grade until dawn. When we break camp, deer step through the woods. A possum glares. In Troy, I search for a wooden horse in empty parking lots while you search for breakfast. At a diner, you watch TV where the new president squints over his florid nose.

"You like him?" I ask, unfolding the map.

"He is an ass hole."

I read aloud about robbers on the bicycle maps and prepare answers, *Robbers equal Robin Hoods, right?* When the server brings your omelet, I ask her, "Have you been to the Jesse James Wax Museum?" She tells us about a cave.

When she leaves to refill your soda, you say, "I will find the Jesse James cave."

Then I ride on lettered roads—M, O, D—and word roads—Church, Commercial, Service. Signs mark waterways—Indiana Camp Creek, Tuque Creek, Missouri River—and advertisements signal industry—government, religion, jewelry. In Union, I snack on canned tuna. On every climb, animal demands of the body preoccupy—thirst, hunger, relief. When civilization markers appear—convenience store, interstate, bridge—I scout for bike racks for Ganga but worry about robbers. Who am I kidding? I've never met a robber.

Day 3
59.3 miles
991 elevation gain

Wright City, MO to Stanton, MO	
November 3	
Temperature (°F)	60/46
Precipitation (inches)	0
Max Wind (MPH)	12
Day Length	10h 28m
Sunrise/Sunset	7:34/6:03
Missouri River & Indian Camp Creek	

At the Katy Trailhead in Marthasville, a gal who looks like a support driver asks, "Will you take our picture?" A trio of cyclists with touring bicycles await. They tell me where they're going—a bike trip on the Katy towards Clinton. She asks, "Where are you headed?"

I say, "Up and down the rivers." Does it matter? Are they robbers? What is a river?

"Oh, yeah?" They nod as if they know. The only part of me that has touched a river is the part of me that holds the bike.

Later, I will call you in Stanton and say, "The Jesse James Wax Museum looks closed."

When you pick me up, you will say, "But the cave was open." You describe it—Jesse James' lockboxes, an underground lake, the sheriff's stakeout location, deceased subterranean creatures, routine EPA tests. I will want to ask why robbers matter, but you will want to talk about the tour guide. "I think he either doesn't trust the government or…."

The word *Or* is a problem.

Tomorrow at the conference, a scholar will say, "All reading is a political act."

Then another scholar will say, "I can't lean on my poem for social change," and, "I've been thinking for some time: What is the work of the poem?"

This will get me stuck between two questions—*Is reading a political act?* or, *What is the work of a bicycle?*

AFTER DOUBLE YY, ANOTHER MISSISSIPPI LEG

After the conference, the *Or* problem persists. We drive towards the route, and nothing calms. Mark Twain's books fail to hold attention. The pile of grading, work emails, and to-dos fails to hold attention. The budget refuses to balance, even with all the attention. We car camp, but your rolling around shakes the chassis. Truck engines growl, *Or, or, or.*

When you get me going on B, near double YY, a detour on D warns, *Bridge out.* Why does Missouri letter its roads? I pedaled D yesterday, right? Will the outed bridge detour me from the Mississippi riverfront?

On D in Stark, more than one spray-painted bicycle marks the town. Each saddle seats a miniature pumpkin. A tandem leads the caravan, and towards the back, a tricycle leaps. In Calumet, where D and N meet, Calumet Creek leads to the Mississippi, ending the detour around the outed bridge to Clarksville. If people are out and about in Clarksville, the town seems closed. **The motel's windows remain dim, the gas station's dark.** At the riverfront park, a woman sits in a car. When she leaves, a man in a truck takes her spot. The locked restrooms and lack of water fountains dissuade lingering. Outside a church, a lone teenager calls, "Hey," but the parking stands chokes with vehicles outside another. I want to meditate, read a good book, or be alone. I ride to find it, but nothing holds my attention, and Ganga's **back wheel thumps** with, *Or, or, or.*

Day 4	
36.3 miles	
1,713 elevation gain	

Louisiana, MO to Paynesville, MO

Daylight Saving

Temperature (°F)	58/44
Precipitation (inches)	0
Max Wind (MPH)	18
Day Length	10h 20m
Sunrise/Sunset	6:37/4:58

Mississippi River, Little Calumet Creek, Calumet Creek, Ramsey Creek, & Little Ramsey Creek

On every climb, the animal body demands. I do everything for relief (porta-potty), hunger (another can of tuna), and thirst (all the water). Then, I start to bonk. I consider waving down random vehicles with, *Water?* but worry they'll think I'm a highway robber. A sign offers, *Duck Eggs.* Do people eat raw duck eggs? At the PO in Paynesville, I check the miles to New Hope.

You arrive, rescuing me with, "Water or sweet potatoes?"

"Ever thought about eating a raw duck egg?"

"What?" you ask, securing Ganga to the bike rack.

We drive towards home, alternating between a lecture series on India—history, Ganges, burial rites in Varanasi—and laptop work. Sometimes it holds our attention. Tomorrow, we teach, dreaming bicycles.

And I'm stuck with *Ors*—*Is the work of a bicycle learning to choose what we'll endure?* or *Is reading about meditation a political act?*—and—*What is the work of a robber?* or, *Are we robbers because we need a getaway?*

TWO SIDES OF THE MISSISSIPPI

The semester keeps going. We grade one project, then another. We teach one module, then the next. We commute through Nebraska's wind. At night, we plan our getaway—river towns, forecasted temperatures, camping sites, breweries. Then, you teach your Monday classes, and I, mine. We attend meetings on teaching technology. Then, like robbers, we take a Thanksgiving leg.

At the Mark Twain Cave, the rope alerts, *Closed.* At an RV park, no one answers the office door. Examining a list of campsites, I ask, "Dupont Reservation?" As the river bluffs climb towards the conservation area, the wheel jerks with the wind. "Or motel?" I ask. What do we need—meditation, laptop work, your favorite beers? Do we work to afford comfort? Or do we ride to be discomforted, then measure the distance between it and the privileges employment offers?

Fall Creek, IL to Louisiana, MO
& Paynesville, MO to Troy, MO

November 22

Temperature (°F)	41/24
Precipitation (inches)	0
Max Wind (MPH)	8
Day Length	9h 52m
Sunrise/Sunset	6:55/4:48

Mississippi River, Cuivre River, Salt River, Guinus Creek, Bryants Creek, & Bobs Creek

Then, I ride the river bluffs. Somewhere, Paynesville awaits with its PO on the road to New Hope. Dogs chase me. Wind tears my vision. Muscles burn. Dormant trees bar overlooks where trucks of men park or arrive, joining me. I return my bottle to its cage and pedal. Many of them wear Carhartt jackets and orange caps, more hunters than robbers. Whose life do they intend to take?

And I ride towards the Mississippi. Near the bridge to Hannibal, a sign directs, *Bicycles must use the right shoulder*, but storm grates and rumble strips eat tires on the bridge. After the bridge, a landscaped mural of Mark Twain's face beams from a hill. Then on Mark Twain Avenue, bookish places alternate with common ones—Mark Twain Dinette, Shell, Clemens Field, BP, Becky Thatchers Diner. Later we will follow a brochure to the whitewashed fences, historic businesses, and literary homes. We will climb Cardiff Hill for Jackson Island's wilderness. At the Mark Twain Brewing Company, you will order a six-pack of Mark Twain to-go.

And I ride with books that discomfort. What causes the discomfort—the audiobook reader, the book, or the cold? When the traffic growls, it robs me of whole paragraphs, sentences, and words. I seek the witness. What story do I tell about this work?

At our river rendezvous, I stretch while you help with Ganga's gear. "You ready for today's last leg?" you ask.

I nod as a vehicle slows. The driver rolls down a window and asks, "Everything alright?"

You tilt your head. I wave.

After she goes, I say, "Midwesterners are so nice," saying nothing about hunters, books, traffic, or cold. As you drive, I meditate for the witness. Then we read your cybersecurity book. You pause it, talking technology—president, Russia, the internet. I listen as we drive towards Paynesville and the day's remaining miles to bike. Cultivating the witness, I note the anxious pinch of my eyes, the pressure in my sinuses, and the capturing thoughts (audiobooks on racial violence, the way rivers wend through a divided city, the rest of the miles). My heart skitters. What might center me?

When her teenage son is shot, she begs the cops, but they stand there.

When I was a teen, we spent one week each summer vacationing in Minnesota—Leech Lake, Itasca, bicycles. The radio played Prairie Home Companion—buttermilk biscuits, ketchup, Lake Woebegone, where all the women are strong.

In the audiobook, all the women must learn to throw punches.

Then, on the road to Troy, the wind punches me. Its cold fist finds my face. I pedal the shoulder—gravel, shattered debris, a dead kitten, desiccated fox. Everything climbs with kickbacks and forks, even the roads—W, KK.

When you pick me up on Cherry Street, you say, "Tell me about your book."

I say, "Tell me what you understand about Michael Brown."

TO THE MOUTH OF THE DES MOINES

Last night over closed laptops, you drank Mark Twain, and me, hot chocolate. If you run out of Mark Twain, who will substitute—Ray Bradbury, Ernest Hemingway, Jean M. Auel?

In the morning, we graded—rough drafts, mid-progress projects, in-class assignments. Tonight, everything will repeat—beer, hot chocolate, laptops. What do we seek?

Today I will ride—twenty, thirty, forty-two, fifty miles. When you check on me, you will talk, NPR and rape—the theft of innocence by sexual assault. Is listening to NPR a political act? Where is the witness?

This afternoon, in Fall Creek, Marblehead, and Quincey, the road and I will shadowbox. Traffic will jeer along a shoulder-less road. A white line will wend through alluvial land, cities, and industries pressed against water. Farms will whiffle smoke as trucks gun the silence of harvested fields. Every rest area will remain padlocked. If the body has needs, they will go unanswered.

This morning when we opened our motel door to go, a gal shuffled past. Then a man did, crooning over what he held, wrapped in his arms. Their door remained ajar, emitting a peculiar smoke. Ambulances arrived as you checked out. As we drove away, you said, "Some woman wouldn't wake up." I bit the rind of a pomegranate, pulling back the flesh to angle it towards the light.

Day 6
50.8 miles
1,059 elevation gain

Fall Creek, IL to Hamilton, IL
November 23

Temperature (°F)	53/30
Precipitation (inches)	0
Max Wind (MPH)	13
Day Length	9h 41m
Sunrise/Sunset	7:02/4:44

Des Moines River, Mississippi River, Cedar Creek, Bluff Canal, & Shuhart Creek

Tonight, when we drive to Keokuk, we will consider sleeping options—Budget Inn, Super 8, Chief Motel—discussing the roadside sign, *Injun Joe*. My high school mascot was a Scarlet, an Indian head, and yours, a horse. How do icons affect the way we read?

And tonight, you will drink Mark Twain, and I hot chocolate. You will click around on social media, and I researching—maps, wiki, town pages. What provokes an off-feeling? I read Mark Twain for extra credit in eleventh grade. You think you read Mark Twain. Which books or poems did we study to learn about the Native Americans and the Mormons? Who is the witness of K12 curriculum?

But first, I've got to ride where the sunset will glimmer pink across the Mississippi in Hamilton, framing a villa. "It's for weddings," you will say. And first, I've got to ride on Warsaw's new asphalt surrounded by grass so perfect, weeds can't poke through, and little dogs in golf carts give chase. Wiki tells, "The mouth of the Des Moines River ends in Warsaw."

Only after that can we hold Mark Twain and hot chocolate in our hands. And Wiki tells— history, inflammatory newspaper, smoldering anti-Mormon faction, people getting shot.

Wiki – on June 27, 1844, "an armed mob with blackened faces stormed Carthage Jail" and shot the Mormon Prophet Joseph Smith and his brother, many times and in the face.

Bicycle map – they "were murdered by a mob of 200 militiamen – their faces painted red…."

Wiki – in a Warsaw tavern afterward, the mob gathered boasting, and all were later acquitted.

Yesterday's audiobook – Michael Brown was shot in the arm four times and in the head twice. His body lay in the street for twenty minutes. The police officer was never indicted.

THE ONCE LARGEST CITY ON THE MISSISSIPPI

Maybe some would rise to family TV and feasts, others to grade to make work disappear, and others to bike. Tonight, after feasts and family TV, we sleep in a **relative**'s house because we know the door code and how to run the washing machine. You stay up with Mark Twain and the TV. I ask, "Will you leave a Mark Twain behind as a thank you for letting us stay?" then climb the stairs for a twin bed that wheezes.

But first, **you grade over the motel's** breakfast, and I ride inside my balaclava and toe covers. I get Hamilton's dawn like I got Hamilton's dusk yesterday. The wedding villa waits with dark windows. A tailwind pushes us on one endless road. The chill stiffens my nose and numbs my fingers, but sunrise shifts the Mississippi's colors—

Day 7
36.3 miles
771 elevation gain

Hamilton, IL to Dallas City, IL	
Thanksgiving	
Temperature (°F)	73/41
Precipitation (inches)	0
Max Wind (MPH)	26
Day Length	9h 40m
Sunrise/Sunset	7:04/4:44
Mississippi River, Riley Creek, & Camp Creek	

gunmetal, turquoise, rose. Inlets edge with cattails, lilies, and weeds. Ducks, geese, and gulls float, skein, and call. Riverside parks hail stopovers with tables, kiosks, and restrooms, but in Nauvoo, signs warn against stopping, loitering, or photographing. Trucks with tinted windows hover. What do they hunt on a Thanksgiving holiday?

We rendezvous in Dallas City, with Lomax still ahead. You point to a massive flag bucking, and ask, "Are you riding to *The Lorax*?"

"Yes, I am," I say. Then the road and tailwind lets me listen to Ganga.

She says, *I speak for the bikes, for the bikes have no tongues.*

Then we rendezvous again, driving to a Thanksgiving gathering. With soft drinks in hand, we feast and family TV. Some of us cavort with games, others cheer for sports, or touch cyber deals and pre-black Friday sales. "Should I buy it?" one asks another. Some talk of a couple's yoga class taught by a Midwest mom robbed of her son. Milk cartons once announced his missing face. "The yoga was cool."

Then, inside our getaway, we number gratefuls. And then I understand why I ride my bike on holidays alongside rivers—to pedal places alone where water palettes shift with the sun. And why I need a map and book as a companion—to know the order of roads and stories that overlay them.

BLACK FRIDAY ON THE MISSISSIPPI, THEN OZARKS

Black Friday will be in three legs.

First, we will lose my sunglasses where dogs chase but find them again near Burlington, the former pearl button capital. You don't wear pearls, but once gave me a strand. Meditation moves me to a happy place, but music moves you there.

Then, I will begin again with *The Lorax* and a tailwind but find aluminum cubes that glimmer with fall. You don't want to shop today, but I ask, "Beer?" Cybersecurity piques your interest, but I remember five-year diaries with aluminum keys.

Finally, I will return to the Ozarks but find a truck hovering behind me, illuminating a path. You don't like after-dark cycling, but we can't control the day's rotation. Some of us need a bicycle as a getaway but grading waits.

First, the sunglasses, dogs with hackles, and pearl button hills begin our pre-dawn.

I search the seat, glove box, and bags but cannot find my sunglasses. Did we leave them with the Mark Twain empties?

"Go. I'll find them," you say, shooing me over the river hills. Minutes later, you pull alongside where I climb, waving their red frames in the air. NPR broadcasts snipe from the getaway radio. You don't say, *You adore me,* but I do.

Day 8
56 miles
2,326 elevation gain

Port Louisa, IA to Muscatine, IA
& Lomax, IL to Burlington, IA
& Stanton, MO to Richwoods, MO

Black Friday

Temperature (°F)	60/32
Precipitation (inches)	0
Max Wind (MPH)	14
Day Length	9h 48m
Sunrise/Sunset	6:58/4:43

Mississippi River, Meramec River, Muscatine Slough, Indian Creek, & Little Indian Creek

"Meet you in Muscatine." Then I roll downhill. In Muscatine, factories billow white plumes, signs urge, *Closed to Thru Traffic*, and workers in fluorescent vests bend with their Black Friday tasks.

Then, *The Lorax*, glittering cubes, and cybersecurity continue it.

The tail pushes seventeen miles an hour until the crosswind at the Mississippi bridge. Grates threaten to eat bicycle tires, and gusts promise to sweep bicycles into the air towards a watery grave. Ganga whispers, *Be careful which way you lean.*

At the exit, a mega-pile of aluminum cubes glimmer. I croon to Ganga, *Oooh, pretty!*

When I get to you, you say, "Oh, a can crusher." The aluminum sunspots. I stretch as you ready Ganga.

We drive. Your cybersecurity book grumbles through the speakers. Turning it down, you tell me cybersecurity will only increase.

I pause the audiobook and ask, "When is it good to have?"

"When it's done the right way."

"What's the right way?"

You chuckle and say, "That's the question."

We drive through the river towns. Every shopping center parking lot chokes with SUVs. We need supplies, but Black Friday keeps us driving. The road becomes a listen to big data—browsers that track search patterns, a *Minority Report*-like future, breakages in cybersecurity. I pause it again and ask, "What can we do?"

"Not much," you say, then restart the story.

Is all reading a political act? Do some intend to keep us cowering? Is the work of a bicycle the moving meditation to learn to note where thoughts and emotions clash?

Finally, the Ozarks, a truck of hunger, and after-dark cycling finish the day.

We part ways in Richwoods, you to make camp and me to climb the Ozarks. As corn-raised Iowans and transplanted Nebraskans, could such hills and twists comfort? I fly downhill, then crawl with grannie gears. Sometimes when a typical Ozark hill appears, I laugh with Ganga, *That's impossible!* then climb it anyway. Sometimes gunshots pass too near where I pedal. *Would they shoot a bicycle?* Sometimes shouldered roads jumble with debris, rumble strips, or roadkill. The sunset blazes salmon. Bats zigzag shadows. I climb uphills of darkness and ride downhills of darkness. I cut switchbacks into darkness and grip the brakes, going into darkness. I hope against headlights that blind, but aim my light searching.

When I see you, you say, "2.5 miles left."

I take the frontage road of silence where the darkness thieves my lights. The air shifts between hot and cold. I coax the bicycle light to offer its **dim waver**. Why **aren't** there streetlights here? The road continues in near darkness, then darkness, then beyond darkness, and **then** it's no longer possible to see.

And then I can see—asphalt, line paint, my shadow I'm chasing. *Adore you,* I think, assuming it's you hovering behind my wheel, illuminating what's left to pedal. I check mirrors, glancing over my shoulder. Headlights fill the road. I think, *What a nice person,* following me and aiming this protective escort to our rendezvous.

I ride with this light for a mile. The only sound is Ganga.

Then I see you ahead. You step from our getaway car. You walk towards me. You take Ganga.

The lights that had been behind me vanish. Not even the ticking of an engine just killed can be heard. On the frontage road, **there's nothing. The witness inside of me gets** bigger, then gets bigger than me. I stand still and peer into the nothing, then lean towards you to give you a long hug of silence.

A security guard approaches, asking, "You guys alright?"

"She's just finishing up a ride," you say, hands tangled in Ganga.

I say nothing. I stretch, and the silence stretches with me.

5,000+ ELEVATION GAIN, AND TWICE OVER THE BIG

I climb Ozarks, un-layering as the heat rises and unraveling over the paper map's direction. We aim for Cape Girardeau in two days, then home for the last weeks of the semester. Will the map ever unfold to our destination?

Day 9
70.6 miles
5,049 elevation gain
Richwoods, MO to Cherokee Pass, MO

November 26	
Temperature (°F)	62/28
Precipitation (inches)	0
Max Wind (MPH)	0
Day Length	9h 46m
Sunrise/Sunset	6:59/4:46

Big River, Flat River, St. Francis River, Little St. Francis River, & Mineral Fork

Today's goal: Richwoods to Cherokee's Pass.

While pedaling, I stare at the map. It undulates with towns—Richwoods, Blackwell, Bonne Terre, Desloge, Park Hills, Leadington, Farmington, Mill Creek, Cherokee Pass. I hunt for cardinal directions on it. Unsigned roads linger with silence.

A number of hills plus a number of climbs equals a factory dissolving of its automotive industry. The audiobook says, *Jobs, jobs, jobs.*

I follow a road that appears to T on the map at Highway E. When I arrive, it's an intersection rather than a T. Highway E lacks a roadside. My aim is Blackwell, but the route becomes senselessness. Does this route contain a three-mile circle on Upper Blackwell Road, Hardin Avenue, and Cole Lake? Or is it circling something else?

Tonight's goal: a cyclist-only hostel in a historic jail.

I pedal. In Bonne Terre, the Highway E sign appears. I track the shifts of name—47, which is also School Street and will become Park Avenue and is also Benham Street which will become K after the highway. And Upper Blackwell Road is also Vo-Tech Road.

Each is also the audiobook of Wisconsin where the GM industry closes. The pen factory closes. Re-education classes open.

At 3:30 AM, I fumbled for the car keys in a tent pocket where you'd stuffed an empty Mark Twain. Mark Twain's dregs dribbled onto your sleeping bag. I aimed: to grade. When Mark Twain said, *Let your vocation be your vacation,* did he mean grading student papers before seven hours of biking?

Morning's goal: Washington State Park's silence for work.

One building illuminated closed restrooms, shut-off showers, disconnected Wi-Fi, and locked ice coolers. While I graded, you folded our beer tent. It's an unsaid silence between us—did you feel me dab you dry, or did you slumber unaware?

In the audiobook, GM offers relocation deals to workers to other American cities. The President provides buyouts to families with unaffordable mortgages. Some of the laid-off go back to community college but using the computer system for enrollment stymies.

I follow the traffic circle near Division Street. Highway 67 growls with heat. My aim is 70 miles and 5,000 feet of elevation gain. Am I climbing the Ozarks, or have the Ozarks climbed inside me?

Today's goal: a local brewery for you and a hostel microwave for me.

While riding, whatever in me that does the thinking blinks at the map, bookmarks, or sips water, but the watcher has left. When I find you in Farmington, it's conversational circles without endpoints.

I say something like, *Food or caffeine, water or bonk, bunk beds or motel,* or maybe *Mark Twain.*

You say something like, *Mark Twain, motel, continental breakfast,* but **maybe it's,** *Another can of tuna?*

In the audiobook, even the newly graduated work to find employment.

I get into the car, and you get into the driver's spot outside the closed jail, our hoped-for bunkbed getaway. Our aim is, *Closed for the season.*

You say, "So, motel it is."

Am I thinking? Or has some multi-named road shifted my thinking?

Today's revised goal: a motel 25 more miles ahead.

While riding, whatever that was left inside me vanishes. At the motel, I say nouns—*shower, meditate, chocolate.* Whatever you say vanishes. Whatever compels talk vanishes. I speak declaratives— *Mark Twain, sweet potatoes, adore you.* Then I rise with a closed-end question, "May I be alone to work?"

One way a bicycle and audiobook works is to let a body alone. At the end of that aloneness, the body wants to be alone.

LAST LEGS TO TEST TO THE MISSISSIPPI

After yesterday's blurred mind, I awake with clarity at 3 AM to the white noise of highway traffic. I grade for five hours. You roll around and dream. At 8 AM, we pack the getaway. Today we aim for Cherokee Pass to Cape Girardeau, then home, then back to work.

Is this it?

I ride into a freezing morning. In the audiobook, all the jobs vanish. The youth get jobs to support their parents until college. Then they must take on student loans, the food pantry must turn away who hungers, and the free health clinic must make a waitlist hundreds of people long.

For miles after Cherokee Pass, the grade eases through coniferous forests into alluvial lands that frame the Mississippi. The Ozarks become farmlands that reach forever. Each town boasts a few hundred residents. After Marquand, a sheepdog charges after me. I shy across the lane, then scooch back over to avoid a truck and continue the work of dodging roadkill—raccoon, possum, armadillo, feline. My grip loosens for the road's vibration.

Near Hurricane, I strip to bare legs and naked fingertips, stuffing pockets and tying the coat in a knot around my waist. Between Scopus and Bufordville, you find me peeling a pomegranate and brushing away spiders and ladybugs. Spiders crawl up. Ladybugs crawl up. Sometimes they open

Day 10
59 miles
3,914 elevation gain

Cherokee Pass, MO to Cape Girardeau, MO

November 27

Temperature (°F)	65/29
Precipitation (inches)	0
Max Wind (MPH)	20
Day Length	9h 52m
Sunrise/Sunset	6:51/4:43

Mississippi River, Castor River, White Water River, Crooked Creek, & Hubble Creek

their shell and fly. You brush them from me. We add the remaining miles. The end of today means tomorrow is work.

In the city, a man steps from a truck, then crosses ahead with a rolling lope, stepping too near my tires. My stomach clenches with a chill. My shoulders stiffen. Is he another hunter in the city? Meanwhile, near our rendezvous, a man calls, "Hey," to you, then his companion lifts her shirt. You turn from them, the pedestrian path, and the Old Mississippi River Bridge to head back to our getaway. If these two walk instead of hunt, why walk that way?

Then I finish the route at the new bridge over the Mississippi. You ready Ganga while I stretch. Sometimes cycling is a dance of *Ors* or a route of *Tos*. Sometimes it's a strip mall of big boxes to fast food to banks promising FDIC. Sometimes it's flood land without a river bridge. Sometimes it's a meditative silence to cultivate the witness. Still, Muscatine, Iowa to Cape Girardeau, Missouri is complete—496 miles over ten days squeezed into the weekends of a semester, plus Thanksgiving break.

In the getaway, we follow one interstate towards St. Louis and another towards Kansas City. For hours, bumper traffic string the interstate, and I grade until it's too dark to grade. Then your audiobook talks cybersecurity over the traffic. Then I say, "Let's take another road."

"Okay," you say. "Help me find it."

FOUND WORK

As children, **we crave** sweets, exciting **games**, recognition, and **attention**. During adolescence, sexuality awakens and **for decades our world is** transformed by it. In middle age, the preservation of family, **work**, or wealth occupies us. As death approaches, **we crave** solace. Find **a** quiet **place to work**. It is best to be alone. Having done the best that we know, we must not despair **if our work** has d**is**appointing results, or is harshly criticized, or **disregarded** altogether. However, when individuals sit down **and** deliberately begin to **work** with the breath, they gradually begin to see changes in the way the body functions and even, in some cases, in its appearance. In **mundane life** there **is** not much time for anything other than **work and** sleep … See all **work** as likable, or at least **find something likeable** about it…Try to view the struggle of **work** as a positive challenge, and the negative experiences as an **exercise** in tolerance and letting go. Many **people** who **work** hard bring their **work home** with them, yapping like a **poodle** at their heels. My life's **work** has been to show how, even from humble beginnings, **this is a path** that can lead the dedicated practitioner to the integration of body, mind, and soul. **We start by working with** the **monsters** in our mind.

WINTER LEGS

Baton Rouge, LA to Bucksnort, TN

Winter Break

Highest/Lowest Temperature (°F)	69/39
Most Precipitation (inches)	1.87
Highest/Lowest Max Wind (MPH)	29/6
Longest/Shortest Day Length	10h 10m/9h 41m
Earliest/Latest Sunrise	6:56/7:01
Earliest/Latest Sunset	4:28/5:07

States: Louisiana, Mississippi, Alabama, & Tennessee

Rivers: Mississippi, Homochitto, Little Buffalo, Yockannookany, Big Black, Tennessee, Green, Buffalo, Duck, Little Buffalo, & Piney

WHAT PARISHES ALONG MISSISSIPPI'S SOUTHERN LEG

As a teen, I wanted to find the places where rivers met oceans, sail with Odysseus, enter the mists to Avalon, and walk with Louis in Anne Rice's New Orleans. Instead, in Des Moines, where two rivers crossed, I washed dishes in a nursing home. To get to any ocean, required books purchased by my part-time wages—used books, grocery paperbacks, thrift store. Then college, part-time this and that. Then graduate school and teaching. Then, while readying for the next graduate program, something about an offer in Louisiana seized my breath and belly. Did I need to know the mouth of the Mississippi? Six months later, Hurricane Katrina landed.

Day 11	
52.7 miles	
1,503 elevation gain	

Baton Rouge, LA to Mississippi State Line

December 16

Temperature (°F)	60/39
Precipitation (inches)	0
Max Wind (MPH)	15
Day Length	10h 10m
Sunrise/Sunset	6:56/5:07

Mississippi River & Thompson Creek

There is a legend about two wolves at the door, one is the wolf of love, and the other is the wolf of hate. The wolf that thrives is the one that's fed.

It takes thirteen years to get to Louisiana. Never mind the last classes, evaluations, and grading. Never mind the last teacher training, team meetings, employment hopes for next year. Never mind sleeping in a rest area where semis grumbled. In the morning outside the capitol in West Baton Rouge Parish, I start our winter leg, saying, "It looks like the capitol in Nebraska."

You say, "It is like the capitol in Nebraska—only taller."

You take a self-guided tour to the top to see where ocean liners hover at the most northern point on the Mississippi.

I ride. ExxonMobil wafts gasses. Rusted pipes pierce the sky with stink. A city park stands with fall-toned trees. Between them on Scenic Highway's two-lane, traffic bares down. We share cracked asphalt, potholes, and uneven gutters. My wheels jerk, focused on the highway path without a shoulder. Engines growl, brushing my legs with a foul heat. My shoulders lock in a grip over the handlebars. Why turn from the place where the ocean suckles the river?

Traffic roars. I keep going, from ExxonMobil, Baton Rouge, one parish, then another. The Mississippi disappears beyond the trees. The highway becomes shouldered, but the glass, sand washouts, and debris sends me skittering among gravel, trash, and animal remains. Then backroads rise with hills—Audubon State Historic Site, Jackson, Wilson, Norwood.

And I read, *Jobs, jobs, jobs.*

And Ganga whispers, *Bicycles don't really change over time. We become more fully bicycle.*

After Thanksgiving break, it took thirteen days to leave Nebraska for winter break. Can we do as planned and continue this route along the Mississippi from Baton Rouge into Tennessee by bicycle? We readied our non-smartphones with audiobooks and podcasts to get away—history, meditation, climate, environment. Will such pedaling continue to disabuse? The number of books I've read about rivers—pollution, cancer, oppression, big business, survival—matches the number of books I've read about love.

I feed one wolf, talking—turtles blinded by fluorocarbons, bayous of toxic waste, unsellable houses on cancer alley. You feed another wolf, detailing—crawdad gumbo, oyster poor-boy, smoked alligator jerky, Cajun frog legs. Later, you will dine with Abita rather than Mark Twain. What beers are named after Louisianan authors? This becomes our road trip game—Anne Rice Stout, Zora Neale Hurston IPA, Kate Chopin Pale Ale.

In graduate school, my advisor asked about my research progress, and once I said, "The best days are those when I can open and close a day inside a book." Biking can be like that—opening with a story and following that story into darkness. What pair of wolves follow?

And Ganga whispers, *We bike the light. We bike the music. We bike the moment as it passes through us.*

The light fades. I ride in darkness. Traffic blinds. My extremities numb with the chill. The low-battery signal blinks, blanking out the bike computer's screen, but I find you at the *Welcome to Mississippi* sign.

The only wolf that appeared all day is the wolf between my legs.

READINGS ON THE HOMOCHITTO

We grade finals until the downpour abates. Then I ride from Natchez, swiping **to the day's** audiobook—southern authors, literary classics, regional nonfiction. The one on pollution, ecology, and politics gnaws with hunger. What's the work of a winter leg? I ask Ganga, *What's our deep story?*

In Natchez, those hidden within vehicles oversee roads in the post-storm glow, but later in Centerville, men stand, sit, or converse in yards. In Natchez, a former plantation with white columns dominates a lawn, but later near Rosetta, trailers and their residents fill the woods. Near Natchez, vehicles scoot into the other lane while passing, but later near the Mississippi border, they ride hard and pass within inches. What rules govern outdoor spaces?

I ride, flying. Spanish moss drapes and trees line the road near Natchez—maples, oaks, ashes, hickories. A half-dozen deer cross, tails raised. Grey squirrels clamber. Birds flit. A box turtle lifts her head from the shoulder. But later near Rosetta, I turn onto Tom Crum Road. It crumbles with broken bits under towering conifers. Humidity lingers, and the insects and birds sing. I might read one book, but the imagery from others layers the pedaling—cotton fields, plantation houses, slave quarters, underground railroads. I might ride through Homochitto National Forest— coniferous forests, soaring trees, landscapes that turn with foliage—calming, but lines from *Native Guard* become mantras. What selfies will await my return to Nebraska?

Day 12
56.8 miles
2,303 elevation gain

Natchez, MS to Mississippi State Line	
Wright Brothers Day	
Temperature (°F)	63/46
Precipitation (inches)	0.87
Max Wind (MPH)	20
Day Length	10h 5m
Sunrise/Sunrise	7:00/5:05
Homochitto River, Little Buffalo River, Second Creek, & Sandy Creek	

In Natchez, signs and highways match the paper map, double checks that ensure I've kept to the route. When the map says, *Opposite old train depot, turn left onto Macedonia Rd,* I do, then near Greenwood Hill, I shed layers, legs half-dumb with yesterday's half-century and the varying road grade—pebbles, broken, faded asphalt. But my wheels waver in Rosetta. I glare at the map. Take this unmarked road? Why name unsigned places? Am I lost? In Centreville, the map's directions garble with roads potholed, broken, and narrow. It directs, *In 0.3 mi., turn right onto unsigned road,* and, *Bear left onto unsigned Camp St. In 0.1 mi., cross SR 24 and right straight onto SR 33.* What does that mean? If some signs signal Crosby, Old Highway 33, and 33, others lack signage. Going one way, then another, I land on 33 and dodge the rumble strips. What stories do the maps we follow create?

For miles, I search the road for any sign of *Welcome to Louisiana.* But when the metal back of *Welcome to Mississippi* appears, I double-back to it. You find me there soon after. "Sorry," you say, "I got sidetracked by grading, then I lost you in Centreville."

"Let's get another map for the Natchez Trace Parkway."

PARALLELING THE MISSISSIPPI, THE NATCHEZ TRACE

Near the Natchez Trace Parkway Terminus, we shake hands to start the day. What will we find here—aggressive drivers or kindness, women who ride their bicycles alone or a community that supports bicycle safety? With blinkers and a bicycle triangle, I pedal the first of what will be 444 miles. Lined by massive trees, the smooth two-lane road arcs through Mississippi. Signs read, *Bicycles May Use Full Lane, 50 MPH,* and, *Historic Marker 1/5 mile.* Vehicles swing around to pass, and my legs find a meditative rhythm. I say to Ganga, *I adore this Trace.*

Outside Jackson, we will end the day with you rolling up beside me with an open window, "You done?"

I croon, "Eighty miles, please," and you give me Dean Stand to Battle of Raymond where you lift Ganga to our getaway, then to the motel. Once we settle, we cuddle, machinating. "Can I do more than eighty tomorrow?"

You say, "It's supposed to rain," or maybe you say to the flip phone, *My wife's on her bike again,* or maybe you sigh, resting on plump pillows.

Near the Trace's points of interest (Emerald Mound, Sunken Trace), we rendezvous, me to refuel, and you to tell stories of the off-Trace destinations (Springfield Plantation, Windsor Ruins, Port Gibson). If a barricade closes one optional site, where beyond it, mud waits to capture getaway tires, we say, "Another time?" With the NPS and bicycle maps of the Trace, I accelerate towards a

Natchez, MS to Jackson, MS

Trace mile makers 0 - 78.3

December 18

Temperature (°F)	63/53
Precipitation (inches)	0.01
Max Wind (MPH)	6
Day Length	10h 5m
Sunrise/Sunset	7:00/5:05

Mississippi River, Castor River, White Water River, Crooked Creek, & Hubble Creek

quick cadence. The Trace parallels the Mississippi along a natural vista that gave historical travelers perspective. The NPS map reads, *Windblown soil (loess) was deposited here during the ice ages.* Near a plantation, a man called to you, "It's private, but people stop here all the time," pointing towards a muddy footpath around the gate beyond where you'd parked the getaway, and you thanked him, keeping the engine running, and hands shifting the gears to ease back to the Trace.

At the National Park Service office at Mount Locust stand, we talk with a couple who volunteer on the Trace. She rolls in the desk chair. He leans against the counter. They tell us about a ladybug infestation, the cranky credit card machine, and their RV retirement. She lectures about the restored plantation and historic house—a bed and breakfast where prior to the steamboat, merchants traveling from Natchez to Nashville stayed here for a meal of corn mush, a mug of milk, and an open-air bed on the porch surrounded by live oaks with boughs where resurrection ferns thrived. Then he tells about bicycle accidents.

"I will give you a vest," he says. He snips the tag from one and offers it—fluorescent, lightweight, with *Be Safe, Be Seen* above a logo of a bicycle. "It's free," he says. "We just need to send them a picture—no name or anything."

"May I have a map, too?"

Later tonight, we will discuss the day's sites and those in our future—Jackson, Tupelo, Nashville, Muscle Shoals—and trace the map, fingers brushing. Does it matter that you tell me we have to grade when I ask, "Can I ride with books as my companions forever?" Which is the wolf that matters? Day three of bicycling still equals strong.

At Mount Locust, we bounce Ganga's tires. "Did you see the self-supported woman cyclist?" you ask. "She's wearing blue." With the NPS map of the Trace and the bicycle map of the Trace, I position them in the pannier case. What do different maps of the same route offer? The road lifts and falls in the expanse of the floodplain, building my strength.

Miles later, she appears pedaling a touring bicycle with panniers to tell about camping alone as a woman—"I dress like a guy. Sometimes I meet people, and they say, 'I thought you were a guy.' And I say, 'Good, that's what you're supposed to think'"—about the hills ahead—"The trace gets hilly in Tennessee. Those are my mountains"—and about her long-distance adventures—"I did the entire Natchez Trace alone in February this year." With red panniers holding everything she needs, her son and husband wait at home in Louisiana. I study the map, tapping the next location of Rocky Springs. Our voices fall into a rhythm until we say goodbye.

At Rocky Springs, we rendezvous to refuel, me for the last of the day's miles, and you to relay information about the ghost town there. When she catches up to us, she disappears towards where she'll camp alone. Later, I will share the details of her life—joining the Katy Trail's annual ride, training in a bicycling touring class, bicycling every long weekend and holiday on her own. I ask, "What's your fare tonight?"

You say, "Lazy Magnolia Southern Pecan," and I pretend I understand the work of a bicycle.

TO KNOW RAIN, MILES OF YOCKANNOOKANY

If I left you to a morning of technology meetings and an excursion to the Civil Rights Museum, you rescue me from a flat on a bridge near Osburn Stand. I release pearls from a pomegranate with wet fingers and kiss your cheek as you check Ganga's tire. Hands bloody with juice, I texted, *Flat. Help, please?* after reaching back and squeezing it. Of course, this is why I'd struggled up the incline. One person checked on me, and a worker in a ground maintenance cart returned my wave.

      Anyone could help, but if a bicycle is my getaway, my home is you.

If the self-supported female cyclist had left me yesterday bemused with her words, "I wasn't sure if it might rain," the first rain finds me on Jackson's bike path that parallels the Trace. Sprinkles merge and slide down naked flesh. I shield the non-smartphone inside my handlebar bag that muffles the story—poverty, abuse, boot camp, secondary education. You texted, *Rendezvous at Cypress Swamp?* after scouting out a bike shop to restock supplies. Of course, the bike path makes the rain playful. The multi-use path curves with sparkles. Park benches glimmer with dew. Water fountains burble music. The etiquette signs make me giggle, pedaling through trails governed by other worldly rules. Two cyclists crouch over carbon bikes. Runners in yellow jackets sprint towards the middle distance.

Day 14
82.8 miles
3,704 elevation gain

Jackson, MS to Kosciusko, MS
Trace mile markers 78.3 - 159.7
December 19

Temperature (°F)	68/50
Precipitation (inches)	0.56
Max Wind (MPH)	17
Day Length	9h 55m
Sunrise/Sunset	7:00/4:56

Yockanookany River, Bogue Ching Creek, White Oak Creek, Pellaphalia Creek, Ninemile Creek, Bain Creek, & Blailock Creek

Anyone could carry a bike from rush hour traffic to an orange barricade that signals a multi-use path. We cross fifty yards for ten miles of protected space.

If I jerry-rig my non-smartphone back into place at Pearl River and the Reservoir Overlook, first the mists, then rain finds my story's unspooling. I shield the electronics with a hand, but when squeezing my gloves releases a stream of water, I pause the story. Driving back to save me from the soaker, you ask, "How are you doing?" after postponing your Civil Rights Museum tour. Of course, Mississippi's downpour penetrates my raincoat, and this is why I hunker, saying, "Shelter?" So heavy and cold, I try to blink the streaming rain from my eyeballs. Among other vehicles at West Florida Boundary, we shiver as the weather app grumbles with thunderstorms of red and green.

Anyone could misunderstand such drumming as, *It's over*, but you still might make your tech meeting and dine on local fare.

If I let the book play too long in the rain, you find me at Cypress Swamp without a functional pause button, asking, "We would call this heavy rain in Nebraska, right?" I quiet the story by the functioning volume button and listen to you describe the walking path between tupelo and cypress.

"Rain makes electronics grumpy," I say, after nudging the volume and sending the speaker snapping. Of course, this is why I leave you to hike a half-mile with your camera. The humidity moistens all—air, skin, clothing—and curls hair. The meeting held between one smartphone (interviewer) and one flip phone (interviewee) left you befuddled over technology, nostalgic for the 1980s.

Anyone could bike the trace with an unstoppable book arguing details, but I daydream of silence. Could I try for one more century this year?

If you find me at Robinson Road, saying, "I saw Santa riding his bicycle," you leave me with, "I think he was going to work." I listen with *oohs* and *ahhs* and ask open-ended questions. You say, "I didn't know Santa was a bicycle commuter in Mississippi." Of course, this is why I keep silent about the contrast between the neatness of the Trace and what lies beyond it. Under a **Trace's bridge** stood another road rutted with potholes and lined by ditches filled with trash, snapped trees, and scrub brush. Near Natchez two days ago, I saw Santa climbing the cement steps to an open porch with grimy siding. He held a red coat in one hand and gripped the railing in the other, baring the essentials—red pants, suspenders, hearty belly, tee-shirt, white beard. I could say, *I saw Santa going into his house,* like you said about the bicycling Santa.

Anyone could make Santa-spotting a road trip competition, but sometimes we win by listening.

If I pedal into the day's expanse of trees and grasses, I find scenes like those in *The Golden Compass* series. I follow the road and imagine I am one of those creatures who'd evolved to roll just here. After inhaling the rain's aftereffects of humidity and exhaling the last of work worries, I *ooh* and *ahh.* Of course, this is why the Trace is magic. Warm air caresses all. An audiobook with Ganga offers a fall-like enchantment on an open road.

Anyone could pedal through such a book, but I get this one for Christmas.

If a truck lingers behind me for half a mile, the occupants yell a bellowing bark as they pass with open windows. I jump and laugh as if goosed. Goosebumps rise. Hairs lift on my scalp. I call, "Merry Christmas," after the truck disappears into the gloaming. Of course, sometimes one road harassment mirrors previous others—trucks with firemen stickers, restored 1980s cars with growling engines, SUVs with tinted windows, lingering.

Any threat could burn, but my support is you.

If we meet at the Kosciusko exit, we find a motel where workers laugh beside massive trucks. You leave me to shower while you seek a fare of shrimp po-boy, onion rings, and southern beer. Workers cavort in your absence. Voices boom. Doors slam. Cigarette smoke slides under the bolted door. I could say how I shook after keeping quiet about the other truck that goosed me. Of course, this is why I say nothing. Ganga's made of an aluminum alloy and if dented, strong. We lift her together. Some men curse and sneer at women bicyclists, and other men catcall and run them from the road.

Anyone could focus on how such men outweigh me, but I want to sleep and tomorrow, bike a century. Is this how the Trace becomes a wolf meditation?

CENTURY LEGS ON THE MISSISSIPPI TRACE

Zero miles – Mississippi's rain deluges the parking lot in Kosciusko. When the winds blow, it slaps all surfaces. Whenever it plunks puddles, Ganga beckons. Then the wind starts again and water drums—vehicles, asphalt, roof. We wait it out. Will a century on the Trace dissolve me? Or, at the end of a century, what remains of a cyclist but the road?

Ten miles – I read about the first woman to bike the world.

Twenty miles – At Cole Creek, I refuel beside a footpath through a swap. Then let a tailwind push me through the hills.

Thirty miles – To your cross-training question, I say, "At the gym, someone else plans the training," and then to your recovery one, "Only men in trucks force me to pedal without a break."

Forty miles – At a sunken section of the Old Trace, we talk logistics: you—birthplaces of Elvis and Oprah—and me—budget and bicycling around the world alone. I say, "Let's use our points for a free

Day 15
100.4 miles
1,578 elevation gain

Kosciusko, MS to Tupelo, MS
Trace mile markers 159.7 - 259.7
December 20

Temperature (°F)	68/51
Precipitation (inches)	1.87
Max Wind (MPH)	23
Day Length	9h 55m
Sunrise/Sunset	7:01/4:57

Yockanookany River, Big Black River, Hurricane Creek, Jaybird Creek, Black Creek, McCurtain Creek, Middle Byway Creek, Phillips Creek, Sewayiah Creek, Prairie Creek, Little Can Creek, Can Creek, Chico Creek, Houlka Creek, Dicks Creek, Chuquatonchee Creek, Sharby Creek, Tallabinneta Creek, Tubbalubba Creek, Chiwapa Creek, Reeds Branch, & Connewah Creek

motel," then add, "She set a Guinness Record."

Fifty miles – With the hills, brush fills the understories of trees. In a gust, a fir collapses. Twigs and pinecones spill across the road. Multi-hued lichen and bark tumble and spread. I ride through the edge of it. What alerts the Trace's crew of accidents—traffic, bicycle, when trees fall?

Sixty miles – I misread the Tombigbee National Forest sign for a residential community. Did I leave the Trace? I pedal hard until the next mile marker's familiar shape. When you appear, I say, "I'm still on the Trace." You ask, "Need anything? We can meet at Witch Dance just ahead." I stare at the map, then cut eyes at the road's endless unfurl. I ask, "Grapes?"

Seventy miles – With doors open, a gal fusses with a children's car seat. A horse neighs from a trailer beside a sign for camping among the trees. We read the Witch Dance sign that says bare grass spots indicate where witches step. You hand me grapes, talking about the strength of women. I say, "If we finish this route, it will be 1,200 miles. She rode 18,000 miles and across four continents."

Eighty miles – Temperatures drop. I edge into Tockshish pull-in where two SUVs meet. Someone gets into one, then someone gets out. Talk syncopates, then silences. Facing the Trace with tense shoulders, I layer, then having finished one book, start another on Katrina. Vehicles vanish, then pass. One driver parks to push buttons on her smartphone. Another fusses with something in the passenger seat, like a century wedged between the cushions. Whatever's inside me vanishes.

Ninety miles – I count the miles to 100 as my book says, *Voice of a storm*. At the Chickasaw Council House sign, you ask, "You okay? More grapes?" I eat them, saying, "She rode 124 a day." You shrug, eyes pinched with stress—job, traffic, job, NPR. "Nine miles left," I say, and name landmarks—Black Belt Overlook, Chiwapa Creek. Then I ride, accelerating into the last of it.

One hundred miles – Near Tupelo, traffic encroaches. Vehicles hover or pass in a string of lights. I sidle onto bridge shoulders but must ride the white line hard. Crosswinds skitter **Ganga's** tires. I brace and wave apologies at drivers. Near Highway 78, a mini-SUV slams on brakes, shimmies back, then swerves again into the oncoming lane. I lift a palm, my nonverbal for, *What did I do wrong?* The driver makes her own nonverbals. Then a state trooper passes. Then a sign appears, *Cyclists may use full lane.* Traffic increases. I ride until the bike computer says century. You are right there.

I am the still point on the road, between biked and yet to bike.

STATES AFTER A CENTURY TO TENNESSEE

Today, you will tour the King's birthplace through Muscle Shoals towards Fame. Today, I will bicycle from Mississippi through Alabama towards Tennessee. I dress in layered kit for the overcast with the bright vest that reads, *Be Safe, Be Seen*. You dress in plaid shorts and a green tee-shirt that reads, *Corn: It's Everything*. Mine hails from the Trace, and yours, a RAGBRAI freebee from the Iowa Corn Council.

"What?" you ask when you catch my stare.

"Is that what you're wearing to meet the King?"

Handing over the maps, you say, "You're easy to find on the Trace."

Is the work of the bicycle discovering the hunger to wander? Or does a bicycle open a door where wolves scratch?

Today, I will take two state line selfies (Mississippi-Alabama, Alabama-Tennessee), study two bodies of water (Lake Lamar Bruce, Bay Springs Lake), follow two waterways (Tennessee, Tennessee-Tombigbee), and cross two bridges (Jamie L. Whitten, John Coffee Memorial).

Today, you will take two musical tours (Muscle Shoals Sound Studio, Elvis Presley Birthplace), study two maps (GPS, NPS), follow two tour guides (recording studio, chapel), and double-back twice or more for me (Jordan Creek, Rock Spring). You dine on BBQ ribs and drink

Day 16
83 miles
1,759 elevation gain

Tupelo, MS to Tennessee State Line
Trace mile markers 259.7 – 341.8
Winter Solstice

Temperature (°F)	55/50
Precipitation (inches)	0
Max Wind (MPH)	14
Day Length	9h 51m
Sunrise/Sunset	6:58/4:50

Tennessee-Tombigbee Waterway, Tennessee River, Kings Creek, Yonab Creek, Penny Creek, Donivan Creek, Jordan Creek, & Buzzard Roost Creek

another Southern Pecan. I dine on fresh fruit (papaya, grapes) and drink electrolytes mixed into coffee. Mine hails from chains, and yours, local fare.

"Kiss the King for me," I say at the Trace, having avoided the worst of Tupelo's rush hour. "This way?" I say, pointing towards where Alabama lies.

"Yes, please."

I ride, easing into an audiobook set in Missouri with visits to familiar towns—Hannibal, Monroe, St. Louis. When the book says, *Monroe,* I remember family stories of work on the levies there. When the book says, *Hannibal,* I remember our legs. What wolf do floods feed?

When the dusk presses against the grey sky, I lose it. Earlier on our mid-route rendezvous, between Elvis and Muscle Shoals, I'd said, "You can leave me. I'm good. Other women do this alone," with a choked bravado as you pulled away, but yesterday's century must've put me in an energy deficit—breathless, heavy-limbed, dull-brained. *Who am I kidding?* I followed the Trace's curves, studied locks, and glimpsed barges gliding on waterways heading towards the mouth of the Mississippi where I've yet to be. At every point of interest—Bear Creek, Freedom Hills Overlook, Buzzard Roost Spring—trucks lingered, pushing me across the interstate or bridges into solitude. When you appear in the glooming, I ask, "How much longer to Tennessee?" in a voice rough with strain.

"Nine or ten miles."

"Which one?" A truck appears. You wave and pass. When you reappear, I ask again, "How much longer?"

"Four or five miles."

"Which one?" We go on like this. Every time you disappear, the hills unravel me—sob, snot, snuffle. Every time you reappear, music pours from the getaway. You silence it, then tell me another pair of numbers stuck between *Or.*

The light leaves the road. The climb never culminates, but the Alabama-Tennessee State Line appears in shadows. I selfie with heavy arms. Then once at the motel, we settle into the calm of research.

Bike map – "The Natchez were the last mound-building tribe in North America…believing that their leader, called the Great Sun, was born of the sun's rays…When he died, all of his wives and court were ceremoniously strangled to join him in the next world."

NPS map – Elizabeth Female Academy Site was "Founded in 1818, first school for women charted by the state of Mississippi."

NPS map – "Most travelers [on the Trace], though, were anonymous working folks."

Bike map – "An assortment of bordellos and saloons, known as Natchez Under the Hill, quickly sprouted to fill the varied needs of the men on the river. The saying soon developed that 'the only thing cheaper in Natchez than a woman's body is a man's life.'"

I close my laptop. "Let's set an intention for the winter solstice."

"What intention?"

"I bike across America self-supported," I say, and the swing of silence moves between us.

Then you say, "I want to practice playing guitar."

LOST WITH CREEKS OF RAIN

The heavy rain sends you out for supplies—groceries, towels, raincoat and pants. I work. When you return, I ask, "Have you seen my speaker?" We search—bags, car, bedclothes, floor—but the non-smartphone speaker has vanished. "We've been robbed." Is this one art? You recheck everything. Housekeeping lingers next door, then the cart passes. The rain pauses, then restarts. I reach behind the dresser, saying, "Found it!"

We load the getaway. You turn on the windshield wipers, asking, "What's this?"

I say, "Rain. Maybe? Is there another word for it here?"

At the Tennessee-Alabama State Line, the mist becomes rain becomes downpour becomes deluge. "Rain must be culture and place specific," I say, naming what's falling around us with Nebraska words—heavy shower, rainstorm, flood warning. I put on the new slicks. "How many miles should I try this?"

"Do they have a drawstring?" you ask. "Do you want rubber bands for the legs?"

"I've never done this before," I say, lifting each limb encased in plastic fabric.

"No one is making you do this." The rain drums the getaway.

"I want to," I say, pushing into a whiteout downpour at a blind crawl. Sometimes it lets up. Sometimes the wind shifts, and it presses harder. Could this test me for biking self-supported? Could I dare to bike through it?

Day 17
22.8 miles
64 elevation gain

Tennessee State Line to Waynesboro, TN
Trace mile markers 341.8 – 364.5

December 22

Temperature (°F)	69/50
Precipitation (inches)	0.03
Max Wind (MPH)	26
Day Length	9h 49m
Sunrise/Sunset	6:55/4:45

Green River, Cypress Creek, & Sweetwater Branch

You drive a few miles ahead and wait. "Are you sure?" you ask when I get there.

"Yes." I dip my head to keep the rain from smacking my eyeballs. When it slackens, what washes from the road channels along its side. The grassy valley of the shoulders runs with a surging creek. Deeper in the hills, streams heave with a rising froth that licks the edges of trees. I pedal for two hours. Every type of rain falls from the sky and runs in runnels down my slicks.

Then at our Glenrock Branch rendezvous, we hunker under the eaves of the comfort station. Water spills against the edges of the free bike-camping along the creek. You hand me grapes. I accept them with stiff fingers. The wet settles into cold. I say, "I'm going to throw in the towel."

"Or get a towel?" you ask. "I bought one for you this morning."

We dash to the getaway. You secure Ganga, then start the engine. Teeth chattering, I fill two plastic sacks with wet gear.

You say, "It's supposed to rain tomorrow."

"You're not helping," I say, rubbing the towel over my goosebumps. You turn up the heat, aiming the vents towards me, then unzip your jacket.

NON-MERRY WEATHER NEAR DUCK DUCK RIVER

If the weather app warned against flash floods— *Turn around and don't drown*—due to the ground saturation—precipitation goes unnamed. Chill replaces the snow, sleet, rain, mist, and fog warnings. In multilayers and reflective gear, Ganga and I push off at dawn. The layers blunt December's teeth. Then it mists. I ask Ganga, *What is this—non-rain?*

Or is this the work of the bicycle—to choose our foes? Or is this the work of wolves—to choose to feed the one who feeds us?

Non-rain mists and sprinkles. It wets the speaker. The book crackles. Non-rain slides down my face and into the jacket collar, darkening the sleeves' hue. The top of my tights grow cold-hot with non-wetness, and my toes chill in the double-layer of non-rain soaked socks. Non-rain moves in sheets across the valleys. It slides over the road. Can I bike fifty miles through this?

To endure it, I wipe condensation from the map case and note the next three landmarks— *stand, old Trace site, five-mile road marker*. Each of the landmarks must be passed before the map can be brushed clean and checked. I climb through the non-rain, then coast downhill through the non-rain. Yesterday's real rain tumbles in brown overflow. It froths and white rapids. It submerges tree trunks and floods farmland and banks. When the glorious moment comes when the map can be flipped

Day 18	
51.9 miles	
1,850 elevation gain	
Little Lot, TN to Waynesboro, TN	
Trace, mile markers 408 – 364.5	
December 23	
Temperature (°F)	69/40
Precipitation (inches)	1.45
Max Wind (MPH)	29
Day Length	9h 41m
Sunrise/Sunset	6:56/4:38
Buffalo River, Duck River, Little Buffalo River, & Blue Buck Creek	

because a panel has been completed, I hoot, *Take that, non-rain!* but when it rips like tissue and lands in the road, I fish it up with tenderness and press it back into its sleeve, whispering, *Love you, non-rain.*

I lean into a hand dryer at the Merriweather Lewis comfort station, warming one thigh, then the other. Later, when we drive back through, you will read aloud the signs near the monument that marks where Merriweather Lewis died. Some sources say suicide by gunshot prompted by opium use. Other sources say, *Unlikely.* Maybe some place trapped him, cold and wet, with a book that kept going. And later, I will read aloud the map—Daniel Boone, Civil War, Trace's history—but when I read the sentence about *relentless Tennessee hills,* you quiet. Needing to feed one wolf (cycling, audiobooks, time to think) rather than another (harassment, weather, hills), I quiet too.

"I'm wet and cold, but I will finish this," I say when you pick me up at the Glenrock Branch sign, adding, "The non-rain has stopped." You drop me off in Little Lot and drive ahead to give me enough miles to make it a half-century. Storm clouds lighten, but the sun remains blocked. A tailwind pushes. I finish one book, and the buttons work enough to start another book on Katrina, this one by a journalist describing a New Orleans hospital. Amid these storms, floods, and hard decisions, I accelerate towards a steady rhythm of breath and cadence.

When I find you, the face of my non-smartphone has shorted out if the book continues to play. I say, "My phone only plays," bouncing on numb legs.

"More?"

"No more non-rain," I say, removing gear from Ganga. "I need a towel."

At the motel, you hand me a fluffy white one. "Want me to run a bath for you?" you ask.

I nod, then meditate, daydreaming of riding a bicycle self-supported. Maybe this is it. Would that be okay?

NON-RAIN'S LAST LEG AT THE FLOODING DUCK

"Does a tailwind work on hills?" I ask. You start me north of the interstate. With the non-rain promising to transform into snow mid-day and Duck River to rise to a 25-feet flood stage, I ride in layers akin to Nebraska commuting gear. Nine days of cycling show. Nothing hides the peppery stink of body odor, streaks of food grime, or stains of road grit. Even the sports bras stink.

Day 19
24.8 miles
1,184 elevation gain

Little Lot, TN to Bucksnort, TN

Christmas Eve

Temperature (°F)	69/40
Precipitation (inches)	1.45
Max Wind (MPH)	29
Day Length	9h 41m
Sunrise/Sunset	6:56/4:38

Piney River & Morgan Creek

Relentless curving hills confuse the body's thermostat. Backroad climbs call for venting zippers and shedding gloves, but downhills freeze the extremities, and non-rain soaks everything—clothing, dormant trees, the road. The grannie gear ascents give ample time to study roadside trash, abandoned businesses, trailers, and houses. Descents to the creeks invite handlebar death-grips. The non-rain falls and falls.

Last night you said, "Ride—that's why we're here." Too non-rainy to read an audiobook, I pedal. The wet roads amplify the heavy traffic. Rumble strips keep me on the shoulder dodging gravel, cracks, overgrowth, and diminishing asphalt, but when I ride the road, vehicles hover with menace, then gun to pass. One jeep blares its horn in a moan. "Merry Christmas Eve," I wave to the driver.

When the non-rain ices, I climb into the getaway, craving—the witness, a good book to read, the comfort of hot chocolate. I say, "Non-rain is mean."

Driving towards Nebraska and our jobs, I calculate the distance of a winter leg—Baton Rouge, Louisiana to Bucksnort, Tennessee. It totals nearly 556 miles in nine days, including the century and one-third of the trip pedaling through bad weather—thunderstorms, heavy rain, cold, snow threat, non-rain. You say, "No one thinks you're not hardcore."

Am I? Or am I just another girl who grew up where two rivers crossed. Why has returning to places where rivers move become an obsession? Am I the wolf?

BEGIN AGAIN

But it is wiser to sit on the ground because, when some degree of deep absorption has been achieved, there is **always a** danger of **fall**ing. But when we're not connected **to** the clarity and **kindness** of presence, we're all too likely to **fall** into **more** mis**understanding, more** conflict, and more distance from others and our own **heart.** Concentrate on **one word at a time,** and let the words slip one after another **into your** consciousness like pearls **falling** into a clear pond. Our **bodies** can **fall** sick, likewise our minds. Simultaneously, you **begin to note** that you don't **fall** asleep (i.e., **fall** out of **the witness**) nearly as often. Throughout the day **you are** remaining centered in the witness watching the drama of **life** unfold. Things **falling** apart is a kind of testing **and also a kind of** healing. We think that the point is to pass the **test** or **to** overcome the problem, but the truth is that things don't really get **solve**d. They come together and they **fall** apart. Then they come together again and **fall** apart again. It's just like that. The healing comes from letting there be room for **all of this** to happen: room for grief, for relief, for misery, **for joy. We are responsible** for our actions; the karmic law of causation tells us that. At the same time, it is also quite true that **life is** changeable, **fleeting,** and illusory. **Great** nations and systems rise and **fall,** people live **and** die, things are **here** and then they **disappear.** When this happens, one or both feet, or even larger portions of the legs, may **fall** asleep.

63

SPRING LEGS

Cape Girardeau, MO to Bucksnort, TN

Spring Break

Highest/Lowest Temperature (°F)	69/28
Most Precipitation (inches)	0
Highest/Lowest Max Wind (MPH)	26/5
Longest/Shortest Day Length	13h/12h
Earliest/Latest Sunrise	6:52/7:07
Earliest/Latest Sunset	7:02/7:15

States: Missouri, Illinois, Kentucky, & Tennessee

Rivers: Mississippi, Cache, Ohio, Cumberland, Tennessee, Harpeth, Duck, & Missouri

A 2X8" FOOTBRIDGE OVER SEN BECK DITCH

For weeks—the rest of winter break, the first half of the new term—sleep eludes. I meditate and practice yoga nidra, anything to give back what's stolen. I am preoccupied with, *Is teaching a political act that disabuses our assumptions?* or *What is the work of a bicycle commuter?* because of the brutality of digits in the teens, black ice, and back-to-back storms tests. Ice and snow sheathe the city. Busses ricochet across the slick roads. We walk or bike, bus or taxi. Sometimes our friends ask, "Do you want a ride?"

But I want—miles, meditate, read, fresh air—and you want—music, museum, craft beer. And the night wind thunders against houses. We commute—classes, meetings, wet bikes, every which way wind, freezing hands—and then we— getaway, car camp, audiobook, grading.

Day 20	
81.5 miles	
1,939 elevation gain	

Cape Girardeau, MO to Golconda, IL

St. Patrick's Day

Temperature (°F)	69/45
Precipitation (inches)	0
Max Wind (MPH)	26
Day Length	12h
Sunrise/Sunset	7:07/7:08

Mississippi River, Cache River, & Ohio River

The spring leg begins with fog at a bridge over the Mississippi. Can we follow the Mississippi from Cape Girardeau to Bucksnort, Tennessee, to complete the river route? If so, what last assumptions of waterways will travel disabuse? Your hold your new smartphone and thumb—St. Patrick's Day events, celebratory green ales, museums. My fingers tap—the handlebars, new smartphone, new smartwatch. Later I will compare digital maps to paper ones. I will save a turtle. I will befriend dogs. Some will lick my face, and others will play fetch. Some will bark, and others guard me against canine gangs. This, like life, goes on and on, all lead-in and prelude, until the next road closed sign. I get pedaling, but soon enough, this sign: *Road closed .4 miles ahead.*

Beyond the barrier, a backhoe, and broken earth, gapes a ten-foot section of removed road. I pace the gap's edge—barriers, re-barb, retaining wall, gravel. How will I complete today's miles? At the foot of the embankment, water braids over mud and rock. Where it deepens to a murky green, water skims over two boards wedged between the banks.

To find the Mississippi and spring break, I must cross this bridge. Do I dare?

Down we go. Gravel skitters. Rocks roll, then plop. Debris mushes. At the water's edge, I test the board. It bows but holds. The water shivers dark green. Across it, the bank rises fifteen feet, shifting with weeds. Like a tightrope walker, a gymnast on a balance bar, or a welder on the I-beam of a skyscraper, as a cyclist with a road bike in her hands I inch across two-by-eights in my clips. Balance. Counterbalance. *Look ahead. Cross this bridge.*

At the other side, a wall of earth. One-handed, I test it like a kitchen counter—one jump, half-turn, and land, bicycle swaying and tangling in—*what?* Yank. Squat. Crawl. Shoulders quiver with burn. What if I drop Ganga and we both tumble into the creek? Sidle in a crouch. Snap twigs. Tug. Unthread the wheels. Free the spokes. Muscles shake. Lean back. The water glimmers, rippling jade. Seesaw the wheels and lift. Legs quiver. Sweat. Reach between legs and underneath the bicycle to one thick root caught on the crank. Unwind it. Eyelids flutter against the water's glare. Then, the pedal frees. Crawl, lift, and drag. Climb through the weeds to the road.

I shake, shuffling through the grass to scrape the cleats clean, then bounces the debris from Ganga, swing a leg over, to begin again.

When I meet you at our rendezvous, you ask, "Anything exciting?"

"Fording a creek?"

FLOOD LINES OF THE OHIO TO THE LAND BETWEEN

Dogs chase, again, loose dogs everywhere—Kentucky, Kansas, Missouri, Illinois. Hills climb, and everything costs. Does a bicycle cost? Or do dogs extract a fee to ride one? Hills, dogs, and jobs make me hunker over Ganga. *Be here and just be here.*

First, hills challenge for thirty miles. Dogs bay. The silver slink of the Ohio ducks. Trash winks. Two mutts skitter me to the road's edge. I dismount, offering a bare hand to their hoary fur. With hackles raised, they drop and half-wag tails. We befriend, but one, then two women in bathrobes call sharp words. The dogs crouch and half-retreat towards them. I remount and ride.

More hills. A blue garage truck passes with stink. A wolf-mix growls for a quarter mile, following. Houses and trash play peek-a-boo in the trees. A hound skunks behind an abandoned building then disappears. And more hills. At one home, trash circles the front porch. At another, trash fills a boat. A Pomeranian-mix hurtles after me as if to yank Ganga from the road and gnaw her to pieces, but when I slide off a glove, she licks my fingertips and shivers as I scratch her mane. A Great Dane with floppy ears bounces through a manicured yard. Still more hills. Trash fills trailers parked in yards. Dogs run chain-link fences, barking. Dogs follow, then mark territorial bushes and trees. At the riverfront, a barricade announces, *Closed*, but unlike yesterday, only dirt coats. The road waits intact. Driftwood piles and hundreds of plastic bottles edge the shoulders in a tangle of flood line.

Day 21	
76.4 miles	
3,622 elevation gain	

Cave-in-Rock, KY to Golden Pond, KY

March 18

Temperature (°F)	45/38
Precipitation (inches)	0
Max Wind (MPH)	10
Day Length	12h 3m
Sunrise/Sunset	6:58/7:02

Ohio River, Cumberland River, Phelps Creek, Cravens Creek, Pisgah Creek, & Long Creek

And all through the hills to The Woodland Trace National Scenic Byway, the audiobooks say, *Work, work, work.* Hello, spring break? At the Welcome Center, mountain bikers circle the parking lot like imaginary creatures—muscle, sinew, dirt. Their gear flashes, fancy, patterned, or spotted. Their bikes splash with color. Some ride fat-tired bikes, mud falling from new tread. Crisscrossing the pavement, thick tires growl like dogs.

And everything costs five dollars. You pay five dollars at the Golden Pond Visitor's Center for the planetarium and tonight's sky. You tell me, "If the clouds clear, I will you show you the stars of Kentucky."

You pay five dollars for the animals in the nature center, where you arrive in time for the snakes and coyotes feeding. The feeder tells you, "The males get frozen rats, and the females get slightly less frozen rats."

You pay five dollars for a six-pack of Saluki dunkledog because you say, "They didn't carry Mark Twain." We pay five dollars to drive through an open range of bison and elk. A herd slows us in their meander across the park loop. Gesturing at the line of vehicles, you tell me, "This is just like Yellowstone."

Warm with the 76 miles and 3,622 feet of elevation gain, I say, "Tomorrow, I'm reading about Iowa to make the Appalachian hills disappear."

"What?" you say, and I know you wonder if this too will cost five dollars.

BETWEEN THE CUMBERLAND AND KENTUCKY

At the roadside motel, men congregate beside trucks with mega tires. Gun racks shadow cab windows. Raucous laughter booms as they drape elbows over truck beds and kick their boots at tire tread. "They've been out there all morning," you say, finger moving the weather radar map when I arrive after biking the first half of the day's miles. The oncoming storm grumbles. You step onto the porch's plastic carpet to guard Ganga. The men lean like robber-kings boasting pillage. You say, "They've been doing that since I dropped you off."

Day 22
50.2 miles
3,123 elevation gain
Golden Pond, KY to Tennessee Ridge, TN
March 19

Temperature (°F)	58/40
Precipitation (inches)	0
Max Wind (MPH)	18
Day Length	12h 6m
Sunrise/Sunset	6:57/7:03

Cumberland River, Tennessee River, Leatherwood Creek, & Cane Creek

Instead of robbers or hunters, I transform them into Huskers. "They're tailgating," I say. "They're corn-hunters and bug-eaters."

"I can't tell if they're going hunting or fishing—what?" You stare.

"Tailgaters."

"You better finish riding," you say as the sky darkens. "I booked tickets," you say, naming them—Grand Old Opry, Johnny Cash Café, the Music Hall of Fame, and a bar called Nudies. "It's the longest bar in the world."

Then the ride zips through red—thunder, rain, mist, sprinkle, drizzle—that pours over the old highway, backroads, and trees bright with spring. Everything blossoms—redbuds, dogwoods, trees, fields. Daffodils bounce in clusters. Homes sprawl, set back between easy climbs and turns. Water soaks through the raincoat, but today's day three, which means strength, and my audiobook

70

gets my goat—*laughlaughlaughlaugh*. Set in my hometown where I commuted to my first part-time job, it dresses the 1950s of Des Moines in humor—packs of kids, toity jars, dinners charred black by busy working mothers—as it considers the peculiarity of Iowa during the Cold War.

Then the ride ends, and forty miles remain total. You wait beside a field of goats. "Adore you," I say, snuggling in for a wet hug, "my old goat."

The goats graze behind the fence, ears flicking. "Are they fainting goats?" you ask.

"Hunting goats." Goats squawk. We load the getaway. You drive towards music, a museum, and a bonus day of riding. I meditate, disappearing into spring break. Could I ride my bike cross-country solo?

SOLO TEST LEG: LAST MILES OF THE NATCHEZ TRACE

What will you do to top that? Graduate school. RAGBRAI. Job. Century. Better job. Headstand. Handstand. Bicycle across the country. At work, does everyone top what came before?

Day 23
66.4 miles
3,665 elevation gain

Kingston Springs, TN to Centerville, TN
Trace mile markers 444 – 408

Vernal Equinox

Temperature (°F)	47/31
Precipitation (inches)	0
Max Wind (MPH)	13
Day Length	13h
Sunrise/Sunset	6:55/7:04

Harpeth River & Duck River

    "Do you live for performance or practice?" I asked my students, and at the door, tally results.

    "Performance," they said, one by one.

    One asked, "What about you?"

    "Practice," I said, opening my hands.

    Then after a seminar on scriptures—*The Bhagavad-Gita, Mahabharata, The Gospels of Thomas*—and after I biked across the country with you driving support, a friend asked, "Would you bike across the country alone?"

    Another friend referenced my work-study abroad in Australia during my first semester as a graduate student. "You did that all by yourself."

    "I did," I said as we carpooled to a yoga class on meditation, neuroscience, and the brain. "I'd forgotten about that."

    Then I researched self-supported cycling—ultra-light gear, bike-packing, tools—and ordered a pannier for Ganga. Shaped like a belly of a grasshopper, it slid beneath her saddle, and there it waited—grading, meetings, workshop sessions—until today. You dress for your musical adventures. I fill the abdomen with supplies. Then we begin our day—you, to live music in a bar and me, to a pre-summer test. Could I? What would a moving meditation reveal to me of stillness?

    Ganga whispers, *No effort in this world is lost or wasted.*

The route slides from city to backroads—farmhouses, horse barns, pastures. At the Natchez Trace Parkway Terminus, historical markers, roadside pull-ins, and services welcome. With an audiobook, I climb into solitude. Non-rain moves in sheets. Another cyclist passes, streamline, forearms on aero bars. At a rest area, I dare the company of two trucks and a lone jogger. I roll into the women's restroom, turn the deadbolt, and put on slicks. It mists, spits, and drizzles non-rain. Without your support arriving until after dark, I number nouns like mantras—non-rain, miles, chill, water bottles, headwind, non-downpour, a can of tuna with a mermaid logo. Then RVs and trucks buzz the rumble stripped highways. Hills force a switchback climb. Then the rain starts. Then it really starts. Then it gets heavier.

Ganga whispers, *Be intent on action, not on the fruits of those action.*

After 66 miles of it and with soggy socks and covered in road grit, I roll Ganga into the motel. We drip a puddle onto the office floor, then get a room all by ourselves. Everything needed waits in the pannier. I peel off the wetness, dropping it into a pile, then shower, refuel, and meditate. When you arrive, I *oooh* and *ahh* over the musical souvenirs. My stories of non-rain, miles, or men in trucks elicit only your nods, as if I've said—*grocery store, commute to work, Nebraska wind.* We must be practicing for when I'll say—*seventy miles of no services, trucks that bounce their chassis' on empty roads,* and, *self-supported century.*

If for a while I pretended, we pedaled in Troy, then *The Lorax*'s weald, then near an ashram somewhere in Iowa, one river kept pushing through it all. We grade. You feast on continental breakfast. You forecast music and beer, and I, forty miles of headwind and cold. I text, *When?* then our swift departure over curving roads. "I'm going to be sick," I say, stomach lurching as the getaway heaves. Shifting across the backseat with gear falling everywhere, I drop between sleep or meditation, deep breathing or silence, daydream, or *I AM*.

When I rise, the hunter goats gather at the fence. A collie-mix trots over. I say, "Hi, Tennessee dog."

"Tailwind," you say.

Again, I pedal forest hills brushed with color. Orange bloom fill trees. Purple brightens the understory of redbuds. Forsythia arches over shoulders. Daffodils rise everywhere. The roads switch with names—White Oak, Greenbrier, Hillcrest, Pumpkin Creek. White-tailed deer leap through hollows. A marmot swims a grassy channel, then scrambles into a pipe. Other dogs appear. One rushes, then blinks at my extended hand. Two smaller ones chase but slow to a halt. *Is that all you got?*

I listen to an audiobook over the last forty miles, like an epic, ten-year odyssey between here and home. Other people grew up reading spiritual texts. Today some grow up reading their smartphones. I grew up reading everything, wandering from paperback to paperback. My path roved

Day 24 40.4 miles 2,503 elevation gain	
Tennessee Ridge, TN to Bucksnort, TN March 21	
Temperature (°F)	50/32
Precipitation (inches)	0
Max Wind (MPH)	16
Day Length	12h 9m
Sunrise/Sunset	6:52/7:02
Tennessee River, Little Richland Creek, Blue Creek, Pumpkin Creek, Hurricane Creek, & Tumbling Creek	

like a river, turning and bending, overflowing in the summers with reading lists of half-priced books. Then, like now, I went to work. I went to school. I read for hours. I planned my route. All the while near my childhood home where the Raccoon River crossed the Des Moines River, the Des Moines River slid beside me, a muted body no one touched. It glimmered like a tarnished mirror. It carried mysterious odors. It divided the city's districts. Where one lived in relationship to it mattered. And this is the work of a bicycle. Rivers braid into something that shimmers with answers. They ferry us to unexpected destinations. They welcome us like a new friend—forgiving, accepting, adventurous.

Then after the county line and last hill, the ride ends at our getaway. "Is the last river leg complete?" you ask.

"For now," I say, "They have a RAGBRAI here, too."

"A bike ride across Tennessee?"

"They call it the BRAT."

ANOTHER BONUS LEG: A SPUR ALONG THE MISSOURI

One more bonus leg. Tomorrow work. The last time we visited St. Louis, we rode to the top of the arch in the alien pods like Martians. Then we circled the botanical gardens and petted Dalmatians at the brewery. "Will you get a big pretzel again?" I ask, shrugging into kit, then ask if you plan to find an STL beer now that STL is no longer occupied. "Do you remember Occupy STL?" Then, tent cities filled inner cities everywhere, even in Nebraska.

> "I need to answer email."

STL's rush hour slides around us with gridlock. You grip the wheel. I zip my jacket to my chin. Then the downtown riverfront drive stands empty near a line of poles with metal flags, caught in a permanent gust. The morning light illuminates—trash, murals, ships, graffiti. One van crawls; a dark blanket stretches over the backseats as he passes. At a crossroads, a mural with a saxophone croons round notes near the arch's silver shape. We pose near it, then shake hands, and say, "Bye."

Chouteau Avenue begins the last challenge of city biking—bike lanes, share rows, side paths, bike trails. Rollers climb between expensive houses on private streets. When the route dead-ends under mega-powerlines at a padlocked gate and a sign warning cyclists away, I double-back and reroute to our Katy Trailhead rendezvous.

> "Sweet potato?"

> "Sweet. Yes, please."

Day 25
59 miles
1,289 elevation gain

St. Louis, MO to Dutzow, MO

Katy Trail mile markers 42.8 – 74

March 22

Temperature (°F)	52/28
Precipitation (inches)	0
Max Wind (MPH)	5
Day Length	12h 12m
Sunrise/Sunset	7:02/7:15

Missouri River & Mississippi River

We talk weather—chill, flurries, headwind. You talk to-dos—groceries, gas, email. I ask about attractions, spring break—National Blues Museum, City Museum, Cardinals, zoo, breweries along the Katy Trail. The traffic into it rolls steady—cyclists, parents with strollers, runners, walkers, dogs.

At the Katy Trail, we squeeze hands, saying, "Bye." I kiss where our fingers touched. Then the switchbacks roll into a silver line of quiet trees and muted shadows. The crushed limestone demands constant work, and everything disappears into the rhythm. This solitude welcomes many. Only the animals sing with chatter. Only what touches the trail caresses with whispers rivers named after states—Mississippi, Missouri, Kentucky, Ohio, Iowa—with colors—White Water, Big Black, Green—animals—Buffalo, Duck—and sound—Des Moines, Meramec, Cuivre, Salt.

I name towns—Weldon Spring, Defiance, Matson, Dutzow—and route markers—a Lewis and Clark route sign, bridges, river bends, open farmland, distant roads. If once gunshots crack in an echo across the water, a thatch of daffodils cheers beside an arrow to a park. The Katy Trail already beckons our return with welcoming silence—deep breathing, moving meditation, a good book. At the end of today, I'll complete 30 miles of the Katy. Is this the work of a bicycle—the permission for quiet? Or is meditation a political act that says, *I am, I am, I am?*

I read my book. Or maybe my book reads me, saying, *belonging, wild, be who you are.* At the trailhead that marks our rendezvous, I could say, *Let's go back to work and home. I'm done with this trail.* Or the Katy could say, *Next holiday break, come back.* Instead, I say to you, "Spring leg complete," helping with Ganga. On the route home, you tell me about your lunch with an STL ale among the talk of locals. I add up what's pedaled—Cape Girardeau, Missouri to Bucksnort, Tennessee—nearly 374 miles in six days. You read. I meditate. And when I rise to you driving our getaway, the only part of me that's touched a river is still my bicycle. My bicycle stills, and that stillness stretches onward.

GREAT RIVERS

Just as the banks of **a river shape** the flow of the water, so does the nasal cavity and upper respiratory passage shape and direct the flow of air. **When the rivers and** air are polluted, **when families and** nations are at war, when **homeless wanderers** fill the highways, these are traditional signs of **a** dark age. Trying to **hurry** grief is like **wanting** a river to stop to our specifications. The river has **to** flow along, subside to a trickle, and finally run its course. If we demand a quick fix or deny our grief, it may **become** submerged in a way that can harm us for years. What about walking along the river? **When a river**, for example, has gained momentum, how hard it **is** to stop it or even divert it! Most of our desires too flow **like** that, along deep channels cut in the mind through **repetition**. But just as a **river can be** rechanneled or dammed, **well-established patterns of behavior** can be changed. **Naturally**, the longer **the channels** have been there, **the more work will** be **needed to** remove them. But it can always **be done**, by **draw**ing on the power released in meditation. Yoga ferried me **across** the **great river** from the bank of ignorance to the shore of knowledge and wisdom.

APPENDICES

CHART: LAND ROUTES & MILEAGE

Day	Date	Land Route	States	Miles	Cum
1	Oct. 26	Burlington, IA to Port Louisa, IA	IA	31.2	31.2
2	All Soul's Day	Wright City, MO to Troy, MO	MO	12.1	43.3
3	Nov. 3	Wright City, MO to Stanton, MO	MO	59.3	102.6
4	Daylight Saving	Louisiana, MO to Paynesville, MO	MO	36.3	138.9
5	Nov. 22	Fall Creek, IL to Troy, MO	IL, MO	57.4	196.3
6	Nov. 23	Fall Creek, IL to Hamilton, IL	IL	50.8	247.1
7	Thanksgiving	Hamilton, IL to Dallas City, IL	IL	36.3	283.4
8	Black Friday	Port Louisa, IA to Richwoods, MO	IA, IL, MO	56	339.4
9	Nov. 26	Richwoods, MO to Cherokee Pass, MO	MO	70.6	410
10	Nov. 27	Cherokee Pass, MO to Cape Girardeau, MO	MO	59	469
11	Dec. 16	Baton Rouge, LA to Mississippi State Line	LA	52.7	521.7
12	Wright Brothers Day	Natchez, MS to Mississippi State Line	MI	56.8	578.5
13	Dec. 18	Natchez, MS to Jackson, MS	MI	80.3	658.8
14	Dec. 19	Jackson, MS to Kosciusko, MS	MI	82.8	741.6
15	Dec. 20	Kosciusko, MS to Tupelo, MS	MI	100.4	842
13	Winter Solstice	Tupelo, MS to Tennessee State Line	MI, AL	83	925
17	Dec. 22	Tennessee State Line to Waynesboro, TN	TN	22.8	947.8
18	Dec. 23	Little Lot, TN to Waynesboro, TN	TN	51.9	999.7
19	Christmas Eve	Little Lot, TN to Bucksnort, TN	TN	24.8	1024.5
20	St. Patrick's Day	Cape Girardeau, MO to Golconda, IL	MO, IL	81.5	1106
21	Mar. 18	Cave-in-Rock, KY to Golden Pond, KY	KY	76.4	1182.4
22	Mar. 19	Golden Pond, KY to Tennessee Ridge, TN	KY, TN	50.2	1232.6
23	Vernal Equinox	Kingston Springs, TN to Centerville, TN	TN	66.4	1299
24	Mar. 22	Tennessee Ridge, TN to Bucksnort, TN	TN	40.4	1339.4
25	Mar. 23	St. Louis, MO to Dutzow, MO	MO	59	1398.4

CHART: RIVERS & WATERWAYS ROUTES

1	Oct. 26	Iowa River, Mississippi River, & Yellow Spring Creek
2	All Soul's Day	Cuivre River & Big Creek
3	Nov. 3	Missouri River & Indian Camp Creek
4	Daylight Saving	Mississippi River, Little Calumet Creek, Calumet Creek, Ramsey Creek, & Little Ramsey Creek
5	Nov. 22	Mississippi River, Cuivre River, Salt River, Guinus Creek, Bryants Creek, & Bobs Creek
6	Nov. 23	Des Moines River, Mississippi River, Cedar Creek, Bluff Canal, & Shuhart Creek
7	Thanksgiving	Mississippi River, Riley Creek, & Camp Creek
8	Black Friday	Mississippi River, Meramec River, Muscatine Slough, Indian Creek, & Little Indian Creek
9	Nov. 26	Big River, Flat River, St. Francis River, Little St. Francis River, & Mineral Fork
11	Nov. 27	Mississippi River, Castor River, White Water River, Crooked Creek, & Hubble Creek
11	Dec. 16	Mississippi River & Thompson Creek
12	Wright Brothers Day	Homochitto River, Little Buffalo River, Second Creek, & Sandy Creek
13	Dec. 18	Mississippi River, Cole Creek, Bayou Pierre, Hickman Creek, & Bakers Creek
14	Dec. 19	Yockanookany River, Bogue Ching Creek, White Oak Creek, Pellaphalia Creek, Ninemile Creek, Bain Creek, & Blailock Creek
15	Dec. 20	Yockanookany River, Big Black River, Hurricane Creek, Jaybird Creek, Black Creek, McCurtain Creek, Middle Byway Creek, Phillips Creek, Sewayiah Creek, Prairie Creek, Little Can Creek, Can Creek, Chico Creek, Houlka Creek, Dicks Creek, Chuquatonchee Creek, Sharby Creek, Tallabinneta Creek, Tubbalubba Creek, Chiwapa Creek, Reeds Branch, & Connewah Creek
13	Winter Solstice	Tennessee-Tombigbee Waterway, Tennessee River, Kings Creek, Yonab Creek, Penny Creek, Donivan Creek, Jordan Creek, & Buzzard Roost Creek
17	Dec. 22	Green River, Cypress Creek, & Sweetwater Branch
18	Dec. 23	Buffalo River, Duck River, Little Buffalo River, & Blue Buck Creek
19	Christmas Eve	Piney River & Morgan Creek
20	St. Patrick's Day	Mississippi River, Cache River, & Ohio River

21	Mar. 18	Ohio River, Cumberland River, Phelps Creek, Cravens Creek, Pisgah Creek, & Long Creek
22	Mar. 19	Cumberland River, Tennessee River, Leatherwood Creek, & Cane Creek
23	Vernal Equinox	Harpeth River & Duck River
24	Mar. 22	Tennessee River, Little Richland Creek, Blue Creek, Pumpkin Creek, Hurricane Creek, & Tumbling Creek
25	Mar. 23	Missouri River & Mississippi River

ACKNOWLEDGMENTS

Thanks to my colleagues and students at the University of Nebraska-Lincoln. A special thanks must go to my husband, Adam Wagler, for his support, love, and generosity.

Thanks to the mapmakers on the local, state, country, and world-level, such as Adventure Cycling Association, Google Maps, and the Rails-to-Trails Conservatory, and those who maintain, support, and protect routes such as the Natchez Trace Parkway, Mississippi River Trail, and many others.

Thanks to the cyclists who ride the bike trails, streets, highways, interstates, and back roads every day. Cycling among these kind, smart, and strong riders has given me the strength to commute year-round, train on an indoor trainer, and venture supported and self-supported farther than I thought bicycles could go. Learning about the bicycling adventures of this community is the inspiration.

NOTES & REFERENCES

Epigraph and Adversaria found poem quotations and notes from the following sources.

Brach, Tara. True Refuge: Finding Peace and Freedom in Your Awakened Heart. New York: Bantam Books, 2013. Print.

Chodron, Pema. *When Things Fall Apart: Heart Advice for Difficult Times.* Boulder, CO: Shambhala, 2016. Print.

Dass, Ram. *Be Here Now.* NY, NY: Crown, 1971. Ebook.

Easwaran, Eknath. *Passage Meditation: A Complete Spiritual Practice.* Tomales, CA: Nilgiri Press, 2016. Print.

Isherwood, Christopher and Swami Prabhavanada. *How to Know God: The Yoga Aphorism of Patanjali.* Hollywood, CA: Vedanta Press, 1981. Print.

Iyengar, B.K.S. *Light on Life.* Rodale, 2005. Ebook.

Kornfield, Jack. "Breathing Meditation." *Insight Timer App.* 2018. Audio.

Rama, Swami, Ballentine, Rudolph, and Hymes, Alan. *Science of Breath: A Practical Guide.* Honesdale, PA: Himalayan Institute Press, 1998. eBook.

Thondup, Tulku. *The Healing Power of Mind: Simple Meditation Exercises for Health, Well-Being, and Enlightenment.* Boulder, CO: Shambhala, 1998. Print.

Salzberg, Sharon. "Breath Meditation." *Insight Timer App.* 2018. Audio.

Sovik, Rolf. *Moving Inward: A Journey to Meditation.* Honesdale, PA: Himalayan Institute Press, 2005. eBook.

Stryker, Rod. *The Four Desires: Creating a Life of Purpose, Happiness, Prosperity, and Freedom.* NY: Delacorte Press, 2011. Ebook.

"A Path": adversaria found poem quotations from Chodron, Dass, Easwaran, Iyengar, Prabhavananda, Isherwood, Patanjali, Salzberg, Sovik, Stryker, and Thondup.

"Found Work": adversaria found poem quotations from Chodron, Dass, Easwaran, Iyengar, Prabhavananda, Isherwood, Patanjali, Rama, Sovik, and Thondup.

"Begin Again": adversaria found poem quotations from Chodron, Dass, Easwaran, Iyengar, Prabhavananda, Isherwood, Patanjali, Sovik, and Thondup.

"Great Rivers": adversaria found poem quotations from Brach, Chodron, Easwaran, Iyengar, Rama, and Thondup.

ABOUT THE AUTHOR

Laura Madeline Wiseman is the author of several collections of poetry, including *Velocipede,* a Foreword INDIES Book of the Year Award Finalist published by Stephen F. Austin State University Press. Other books of poetry include *What a Bicycle Can Carry, Through a Certain Forest, An Apparently Impossible Adventure, Wake, Some Fatal Effects of Curiosity and Disobedience, Sprung, American Galactic,* and *Queen of the Platform.* Her newest poetry book is *Journey to Nowhere* from Finishing Line Press. Her newest chapbook of poetry is *Diversions* from Dancing Girl Press.

Madeline has collaborated on books with writers, artists, designers, and illustrators, including *Intimates and Fools* and *Leaves of Absence,* both with Sally Deskins. Other collaborative books include *People Like Cats* and *The Hunger of the Cheeky Sisters.* Her newest collaborative chapbook is *Every Girl Becomes the Wolf* with Andrea Blythe, published by Finishing Line Press. She edited two poetry anthologies, *Bared: Contemporary Poetry and Art on Bras and Breasts* and *Women Write Resistance: Poets Resist Gender Violence.* She is the editor of *The Chapbook Interview.*

Madeline is also the author of prose. Her collection of creative nonfiction is *A Bicycle's Echo* published by Red Dashboard. Her newest lyric prose collection is *Safety Measures* published by Zea Books. Her poetry, fiction, nonfiction, and reviews have appeared in *Margie, Mid-American Review, Poet Lore, Blackbird, Arts & Letters, Prairie Schooner, Feminist Studies, The Iowa Review, Ploughshares,* and *Calyx.*

Madeline earned a B.S. in Women's Studies and English Literature from Iowa State University, an M.A. in Women's Studies from the University of Arizona, and a Ph.D. in English the University of Nebraska-Lincoln. She recently earned a second M.A. in Integrated Media Communications from the University of Nebraska-Lincoln.

She has received an Academy of American Poets Award, a Louise Van Sickle Fellowship, the Helene Wurlitzer Foundation Fellowship, a Hitchcock Fellowship, and grants from the Kimmel Harding Nelson Center for the Arts and the Center for the Great Plains Studies.

ALSO BY THE AUTHOR

Books

Safety Measures (Zea Books, 2021)

Journey to Nowhere (Finishing Line Press, 2019)

What a Bicycle Can Carry (BlazeVOX [books], 2018)

A Bicycle's Echo (Red Dashboard, 2018)

Through a Certain Forest (BlazeVOX [books], 2017)

Velocipede (Stephen F. Austin State University Press, 2016)

An Apparently Impossible Adventure (BlazeVOX [books], 2016)

Drink (BlazeVOX [books], 2015)

Wake (Aldrich Press, 2015)

American Galactic (Martian Lit Books, 2014)

Some Fatal Effects of Curiosity and Disobedience (Lavender Ink, 2014)

Queen of the Platform (Anaphora Literary Press, 2013)

Sprung (San Francisco Bay Press, 2012)

Collaborative Collections

Yoga Birds with designer Adam Wagler (Zea Books, 2019)

Every Girl Becomes the Wolf with poet Andrea Blythe (Finishing Line Press, 2018)

People like Cats with artist Chuka Susan Chesney (Red Dashboard, 2016)

Leaves of Absence: An Illustrated Guide to Common Garden Affection with artist Sally Deskins
    (Red Dashboard, 2016)

The Hunger of the Cheeky Sisters: Ten Tales with artist Lauren Rinaldi
    (Les Femmes Folles Books, 2015)

Intimates and Fools with artist Sally Deskins (Les Femmes Folles Books, 2014)

Edited Collections

Bared: Contemporary Poetry and Art on Bras and Breasts (Les Femmes Folles Books, 2017)

Women Write Resistance: Poets Resist Gender Violence (Hyacinth Girl Press, 2013)

Letterpress Collections

Unclose the Door (Gold Quoin Press, 2012)

Farm Hands (Gold Quoin Press, 2012)

Chapbooks

Diversions (Dancing Girl Press, 2019)

Threnody (Porkbelly Press, 2014)

The Bottle Opener (Red Dashboard, 2014)

Spindrift (Dancing Girl Press, 2014)

Stranger Still (Finishing Line Press, 2013)

First Wife (Hyacinth Girl Press, 2013)

Men and Their Whims (Writing Knights Press, 2013)

She Who Loves Her Father (Dancing Girl Press, 2012)

Branding Girls (Finishing Line Press, 2011)

Ghost Girl (Pudding House, 2010)

My Imaginary (Dancing Girl Press, 2010)

www.ingramcontent.com/pod-product-compliance
Lightning Source LLC
Chambersburg PA
CBHW081517040426

42447CB00013B/3249